CW00924271

The Book of Mansur Hallaj

Selected Poems & Tasawin

The Book of Mansur Hallaj

Selected Poems & Tawasin

Translations and Introduction

Paul Smith

NEW HUMANITY BOOKS
Book Heaven
Booksellers & Publishers

Copyright © Paul Smith 2012, 2014

NEW HUMANITY BOOKS
BOOK HEAVEN
(Booksellers & Publishers for over 40 years)
47 Main Road Campbells Creek
Victoria, 3450 Australia

www.newhumanitybookbookheaven.com

ISBN: 978-1500508845

The Torture of Hallaj 'to relieve him of his demons'.

>CONTENTS<

The Life, Times and Works of Mansur Hallaj... page 7

Selected Bibliography... 18

The Perfect Master (Qutub)... 19

'Anal-Haqq' or 'I am the Truth' of Mansur Hallaj... 29

Four Master Poets of Baghdad who influenced Hallaj... 35

Sufis & Dervishes: Their Art & Use of Poetry... 71

Qit'as... 75

Ghazals... 125

Ruba'is... 135

Qasidas... 143

THE TAWASIN... 149

Appendix:

The Story of Iblis (Azazil) and Adam
From 'The Book of Genesis'
of Shahin of Shiraz ... 319

The Life, Times and Works of Mansur Hallaj.

Husayn Mansur al-Hallaj (859-922) was a Perfect Master *(Qutub)* and a poet who was born near Shiraz (Bayda), Persia... a writer and teacher of Sufism most famous for his self-proclaimed divinity in his poetry and for his execution for heresy at the hands of the Abbasid rulers. Although Hallaj was born in Persia and was of Persian descent, he wrote most of his works in Arabic.

He married and had three children and made a pilgrimage to Mecca, stayed for one year, facing the mosque, in fasting and total silence. After his stay at the city, he travelled extensively and wrote and taught along the way. He travelled as far as India and Central Asia gaining many followers, many of whom accompanied him on his second and third trips to Mecca. After this period of travel, he settled in the capital of Baghdad.

During his early lifetime he was a disciple of Junaid and Amr al-Makki, but was later rejected by them both. Among other Sufis, Hallaj was an anomaly. Many Sufi masters felt that it was inappropriate to share his inner experiences with the masses, yet Mansur Hallaj openly did so in his writings and through his teachings. He began to make enemies, and the rulers saw him as a threat. This was exacerbated by times when he would fall into trances that he attributed to being in the presence of God. During one of these trances, he would utter *Anal-Haqq* literally meaning, "I am the Absolute Truth", which was taken to mean that he was claiming to be God. In another controversial statement, Hallaj claimed: "There is nothing wrapped in my turban but

God," and, again, similarly, he would point to his cloak and say, "There is nothing inside my cloak except God."

These utterances led him to a long trial, and subsequent imprisonment for eleven years in a Baghdad prison. In the end, he was tortured and publicly crucified (in some accounts he was beheaded and his hands and feet were cut off) by the Abbasid rulers for what they deemed 'theological error threatening the security of the state.' Many accounts tell of Hallaj's calm demeanour even while he was being tortured, and indicate that he forgave those who had executed him. He was executed on March 26, 922. It is said that while he was savagely tortured before he was killed he kept calling out: *"Anal Haqq!"*

It is also reported that after his body was burnt and the ashes thrown into the Tigris River they spelt out the words *"Anal Haqq!"* His influence on all Sufis, be they poets or not, who have come after him, cannot be overestimated. (See Appendix).

Apart from the many books and poems that have been written and inspired by Sufism's greatest martyr in the past hundred years there have also been a number of plays and films and even puppet shows about his life and in particular his terrible death.

A Recent Play   An Iranian Puppet Play

Farid-ud-din 'Attar in his *Tazkirat-ul-Aulia (Muslim, Saints and Mystics)* says of him as follows:

"This is he who was a martyr in the way of truth, whose rank has become exalted, whose outer and inner man were pure, who has been a pattern of loyalty in love, whom an irresistible longing drew towards the contemplation of the face of God; this is the enthusiast Mansur Hallaj, may the mercy of God be upon him! He was intoxicated with a love whose flames consumed him. The miracles he worked were such that the learned were thunderstruck at them. He was a man whose range of vision was immense, whose words were riddles, and profoundly versed in the knowledge of mysteries. Born in the canton of Bayda in the province of Shiraz, he grew up at Wasit.

Abd Allah Khafif used to say, 'Mansur really possessed the knowledge of the truth.' 'I and Mansur,' declared Shibli, 'followed the same path; they regarded me as mad and my life was saved thereby, while Mansur perished because he was sane.' If Mansur had been really astray in error, the two learned men we have just quoted would not have spoken of him in such terms. Many wise men, however, have reproached him for revealing the mysteries of truth to the vulgar herd.

When he had grown up, he was two years in the service of Abd Allah Teshtari. He made the pilgrimage to Mecca, and on his return became a disciple of the Sufi Junaid. One day, when Mansur was plying him with questions on certain obscure and difficult points, Junaid said, 'O Mansur, before very long you will redden the head of the stake.'

'The day when I redden the head of the stake,' rejoined Mansur, 'you will cast away the garment of the dervish and assume that of ordinary men.' It is related that on the day when Mansur was taken to execution all the Ulama (head priests) signed the sentence of death. 'Junaid also must sign,' said the Caliph. Junaid accordingly repaired to the college of the Ulama, where, after putting on a mullah's robe and turban, he recorded in writing his opinion that 'though apparently Mansur deserved death, inwardly he possessed the knowledge of the Most High.'

Having left Bagdad, Mansur spent a year at Tashter, then he spent five years in travelling through Khorassan, Seistan and Turkestan. On his return to Bagdad, the number of his followers largely increased, and he gave utterance to many strange sayings which excited the suspicions of the orthodox. At last he began to say, 'I am the Truth.' These words were repeated to the Caliph and many persons renounced Mansur as a religious leader and appeared as witnesses against him. Among these was Junaid, to whom the Caliph said, 'O Junaid, what is the meaning of this saying of Mansur?' 'O Caliph,' answered Junaid, 'this man should be put to death, for such a saying cannot be reasonably explained.' The Caliph then ordered him to be cast into prison. There for a whole year he continued to hold discussions with the learned. At the end of that time the Caliph forbade that anyone should have access to him; in consequence, no one went to see him for five months except Abd Allah Khafif. Another time Ibn Ata sent someone to say to him, 'O Sheikh, withdraw what you said, so that you may escape death.' 'No, rather he who sent you to me should ask forgiveness,' replied Mansur. Ibn Ata, hearing this, shed tears and said, 'Alas, he is irreparably lost!'

In order to force him to retract, he was first of all given three hundred blows with a rod, but in vain. He was then led to execution. A crowd of about a hundred thousand men followed him and as he looked around on them, he cried, 'True! True! True! I am the Truth!'

It is said that among them was a dervish who asked him, 'What is love?'

'You will see,' Mansur replied, 'to-day and to-morrow and the day after.' And as it happened, that day he was put to death, the next day his body was burnt and on the third his ashes were scattered to the winds. He meant that such would be the results of his love to God. On his son asking of him a last piece of advice he said, 'While the people of the world spend their energies on earthly objects, you apply yourself to a study, the least portion of which is worth all that men and *jinn* can produce… the study of truth.'

As he walked along lightly and alertly, though loaded with many chains, they asked him the reason of his confident bearing. 'It is,' he said, 'because I am going to the presence of the King.' Then he added, 'My Host, in whom there is no injustice, has presented me with the drink which is usually given to a guest; but when the cups have began to circulate he has sent for the executioner with his sword and leathern carpet. Thus fares it with him who drinks with the Dragon in July.'

When he reached the scaffold, he turned his face towards the western gate of Bagdad and set his foot on the first rung of the ladder, 'the first step heavenward,' as he said. Then he girded himself with a girdle, and, lifting up his hands towards heaven, turned towards Mecca, and said exultantly, 'Let it be as He has willed.' When he reached the platform of the scaffold, a group of his disciples called out to him, 'What do you say regarding us, your disciples, and regarding those who deny your claims and are about to stone you?' 'They will have a two-fold reward, and you only a single one,' he answered, 'for you limit yourselves to having a good opinion of me, while they are carried on by their zeal for the unity of God and for the written law. Now in the law the doctrine of God's unity is fundamental, while a good opinion is merely accessory.'

Shibli the Sufi stood in front of him and cried, 'Did we not tell you not to gather men together?' Then he added, 'O Hallaj, what is Sufism?' 'Thou see,' replied Hallaj, 'the least part of it.' 'What is then the highest?' asked Shibli. 'You cannot attain to it,' he answered.

Then they all began to stone him. Shibli making common cause with the others threw mud at him. Hallaj uttered a cry. 'What,' said one, 'you have not flinched under this hail of stones and now you cry out because of a little mud! Why is that?' 'Ah!' he replied, 'they do not know what they are doing, and are excusable; but he grieves me because he knows I ought not to be stoned at all.'

When they cut off his hands he laughed and said, 'To cut off the hands of a fettered man is easy, but to sever the links which bind me to the Divinity would be a task indeed.' Then they cut off his two feet. He said smiling, 'With these I used to accomplish my earthly journeys, but I have another pair of feet with which I can traverse both worlds. Cut these off if you can!' Then, with his bleeding stumps, he rubbed his cheeks and arms. 'Why do you do that?' he was asked. 'I have lost much blood,' he answered, 'and lest you should think the pallor of my countenance shows fear, I have reddened my cheeks.' 'But why your arms?' 'The ablutions of love must be made in blood,' he replied.

Then his eyes were torn out. At this a tumult arose in the crowd. Some burst into tears, others cast stones at him. When they were about to cut out his tongue, he exclaimed, 'Wait a little; I have something to say.'

Then, lifting his face towards heaven, he said, 'My God, for the sake of these sufferings, which they inflict on me because of You, do not inflict loss upon them nor deprive them of their share of felicity. Behold, upon the scaffold of my torture I enjoy the contemplation of Your glory.' His last words were, 'Help me, O You only One, to whom there is no second!' and he recited the following verse of the *Koran*, 'Those who do not believe say, "Why does not the day of judgment hasten? Those who believe tremble at the mention of it, for they know that it is near."' Then they cut out his tongue, and he smiled. Finally, at the time of evening prayer, his head was cut off. His body was burnt, and the ashes thrown into the Tigris."

Translated by Claud Field in his *Mystics & Saints of Islam*, Francis Griffiths, London, 1910.

Abu 'l-Hasan al-Hujwiri (d. 1072) one of the most respected early authors on Sufism states in his *Kashf al-Mahjub* as translated by R.A. Nicholson... "He was an enamoured and intoxicated votary of Sufism. He had a strong ecstasy and a lofty spirit. The Sufi Shaykhs are at variance concerning him. Some reject him, while others accept him. Among the latter class are He was an enamoured and intoxicated votary of Sufism. Among the latter class are Amr b. Uthman al- Makki, Abu Ya'qub Nahrajuri, Abu Ya'qub Aqta', Ali b. Sahl Isfahani, and others. He is accepted, moreover, by Ibn 'Ata, Muhammad b. Khafif, Abu 'l-Qasim Nasrabadi, and all the moderns. Others, again, suspend their judgment about him, e.g. Junayd and Shibli and Jurayri and Husri. Some accuse him of magic and matters coming under that head, but in our days the Grand Shaykh Abu Sa'id b. Abu 'l-Khayr and Shaykh Abu 'l-Qasim Gurgani and Shaykh Abu 'l- Abbas Shaqani looked upon him with favour, and in their eyes he was a great man. The Master Abu 'l-Qasim Qushayri remarks that if al-Hallaj was a genuine spiritualist he is not to be banned on the ground of popular condemnation, and if he was banned by Sufism and rejected by the Truth he is not to be approved on the ground of popular approval. Therefore we leave him to the judgment of God, and honour him according to the tokens of the Truth which we have found him to possess. But of all these Shaykhs only a few deny the perfection of his merit and the purity of his spiritual state and the abundance of his ascetic practices. It would be an act of dishonesty to omit his biography from this book. Some persons pronounce his outward behaviour to be that of an infidel, and disbelieve in him and charge him with trickery and magic, and suppose that Husayn b. Mansur Hallaj is that heretic of Baghdad who was the master of Muhammad b. Zakariyya and the companion of Abu Sa'id the Carmathian; but this Husayn whose character is in dispute was a Persian and a native of Bayda (near Shiraz), and his rejection by the Shaykhs was due, not to any attack on religion and doctrine, but to his conduct and behaviour. At first he was a pupil of Sahl b. 'Abdallah, whom he left, without asking permission, in order to attach himself to Amr b. Uthman Makki. Then he left Amr b. Uthman, again without asking permission, and sought to associate with Junayd, but Junayd would not receive him. This is the reason why he is banned by all the Shaykhs. Now, one who is banned on account of his conduct is not banned on account of his principles. Do you not see that Shibli said: 'Al-Hallaj and I are of one belief, but my madness saved me, while his intelligence destroyed him?' Had his religion been suspected, Shibli would not have said: 'Al-Hallaj and I are of one belief.' And Muhammad b. Khafif said: 'He is a divinely learned man' (alim-i rabbani). Al-Hallaj is the author of brilliant compositions and allegories and polished sayings in theology and jurisprudence. I have seen fifty works by him at Baghdad and in the neighbouring districts, and some in Khuzistan and Fars and Khurasan. All his sayings are like the first visions of novices; some of them are stronger, some weaker, some easier, some more unseemly than others. When God bestows a vision on anyone, and he endeavours to describe what he has seen with the power of ecstasy and the help of Divine grace, his words are obscure, especially if he expresses himself with haste and self-admiration: then they are more repugnant to the imaginations, and incomprehensible to the minds, of those who hear them, and then people say, 'This is a sublime utterance,' either believing it or not, but equally ignorant of its meaning whether they believe or deny. On the other hand, when persons of true spirituality and insight have visions, they make no effort to describe them, and do not occupy themselves with self-admiration on that account, and are careless of praise and blame alike, and are undisturbed by denial and belief.

It is absurd to charge al-Hallaj with being a magician. According to the principles of Muhammadan orthodoxy, magic is real, just as miracles are real; but the manifestation of magic in the state of perfection is infidelity, whereas the manifestation of miracles in the state of perfection is knowledge of God (*ma'rifat*), because the former is the result of God's anger, while the latter is the corollary of His being well pleased. I will explain this more fully in the chapter on the affirmation of miracles. By consent of all Sunnites who are endowed with perspicacity, no Moslem can be a magician and no infidel can be held in honour, for contraries never meet. Husayn, as long as he lived, wore the garb of piety, consisting in prayer and praise of God and continual fasts and fine sayings on the subject of Unification. If his actions were magic, all this could not possibly have proceeded from him. Consequently, they must have been miracles, and miracles are vouchsafed only to a true saint. Some orthodox theologians reject him on the ground that his sayings are pantheistic (*ba-ma'ni-yi imtizaj u ittihad*), but the offence lies solely in the expression, not in the meaning. A person overcome with rapture has not the power of expressing himself correctly; besides, the meaning of the expression may be difficult to apprehend, so that people mistake the writer's intention, and repudiate, not his real meaning, but a notion which they have formed for themselves. I have seen at Baghdad and in the adjoining districts a number of heretics who pretend to be the followers of al-Hallaj and make his sayings an argument for their heresy (*zandaqa*) and call themselves Hallajis. They spoke of him in the same terms of exaggeration (*ghuluww*) as the Rafidis (Shi'ites) apply to 'Ali. I will refute their doctrines in the chapter concerning the different Sufi sects.

In conclusion, you must know that the sayings of al-Hallaj should not be taken as a model, inasmuch as he was an ecstatic *(maghlub andar hal-i khud)*, not firmly settled *(mutamakkin)* and a man needs to be firmly settled before his sayings can be considered authoritative. Therefore, although he is dear to my heart, yet his 'path' is not soundly established on any principle, and his state is not fixed in any position, and his experiences are largely mingled with error. When my own visions began I derived much support from him, that is to say, in the way of evidences *(barahin)*. At an earlier time I composed a book in explanation of his sayings and demonstrated their sublimity by proofs and arguments. Furthermore, in another work, entitled *Minhaj*, I have spoken of his life from beginning to end; and now I have given some account of him in this place. How can a doctrine whose principles require to be corroborated with so much caution be followed and imitated? Truth and idle fancy never agree. He is continually seeking to fasten upon some erroneous theory. It is related that he said: *Al-alsinat mustan- tiqdt tahta nutqiha mustahlikat,* i.e. 'speaking tongues are the destruction of silent hearts'. Such expressions are entirely mischievous. Expression of the meaning of reality is futile. If the meaning exists it is not lost by expression, and if it is non-existent it is not created by expression."

SELECTED BIBLIOGRAPHY

Divan al-Hallaj: Kamil M. Shaibi, Baghdad, 1974.

Mansur Hallaj: Selected Poems, Translation & Introduction Paul Smith, New Humanity Books, Campbells Creek, 2012.

The Tawasin: Mansur Hallaj Translation & Introduction by Paul Smith, New Humanity Books, Campbells Creek, 2013.

The Passion of al-Hallaj by Louis Massignon, 4 vols, Trans. by Herbert Mason, Princeton University Press 1983.

Hallaj: Mystic and Martyr, by Louis Massignon, Translated, edited abridged by Herbert Mason. Princeton University Press. 1994.

Al-Hallaj. Herbert W. Mason. Curzon Press, Surrey, 1995.

The Tawasin of Mansur al-Hallaj, Translated by Aisha Abd Ar-Rahman At-Tarumana, Diwan Press, Berkeley, 1974.

Sufi Poems, A Mediaeval Anthology by Martin Lings, Islamic Texts Society, Cambridge, 2004. (Pages 26-41).

A Critical Appreciation of Arabic Mystical Poetry by Dr. S.H. Nadeem, Adam Pub. New Delhi, 2003. (Pages 53-71.)

Islamic Mystical Poetry: Sufi Verse from the Early Mystics to Rumi, Edited with translations and introduction by Mahmood Jamal, Penguin Books, London. (Pages 13-34).

The Way of the Mystics: The Early Christian Mystics and the Rise of the Sufis by Margaret Smith… reprint Sheldon Press 1976.

Hallaj: Poemes mystiques, Trans. etc., Sami-Ali, Sindbad, Arles, 1985.

Muslim Saints and Mystics… Episodes from the Tadhkirat al-Auliya' (The Lives of the Saints) by Farid al-Din 'Attar Translated by A.J. Arberry. Routledge & Kegan Paul 1966. (Pages 264-272).

Kashf Al-Mahjub of Al-Hujwiri: The Oldest Persian Treatise on Sufism By 'Ali B. 'Uthman Al-Jullani Al-Hujwiri, Translated by Reynold A. Nicholson, Luzac & Co. London 1911. (Pages 50-53 et al).

Reorientations/Arabic and Persian Poetry Edited by Suzanne Pinckney Stetkevych, Indiana University Press, 1994. (Pages 93-94).

The Idea of Personality in Sufism by Reynold Alleyne Nicholson, Cambridge, 1923 (Pages 27-37).

The Death of al-Hallaj: A Dramatic Narrative by Herbert Mason, University of Notre Dame Press, 1979.

The Tawasin of Mansur al-Hallaj: Interpreted in Poetry by Jabez L. Van Cleef, Spirit Son Text, New Jersey, 2008. (In masnavi form).

The Perfect Master (Qutub).

Mansur al-Hallaj is considered by many of the greatest poets and Masters of Sufism to have been a God-realized soul, a Perfect Master (Qutub). I will now try to define God-realization and the clearest and best definition that I know is that by Meher Baba in *Discourses* Sufism Reoriented, San Francisco 6th Edition 1967: "To arrive at true self-knowledge is to arrive at God-realisation. God-realisation is a unique state of consciousness. It is different from all the other states of consciousness because all the other states of consciousness are experienced through the medium of the individual mind; whereas the state of God-consciousness is in no way dependent upon the individual mind or any other medium. A medium is necessary for knowing something other than one's own self. For knowing one's own self no medium is necessary. In fact, the association of consciousness with the mind is definitely a hindrance rather than a help for the attainment of realisation. The individual mind is the seat of the ego or the consciousness of being isolated. It creates the limited individuality, which at once feeds on and is fed by the illusion of duality, time and change. So, in order to know the Self as it is, consciousness has to be completely freed from the limitation of the individual mind. In other words, the individual mind has to disappear but consciousness has to be retained... The consciousness which was hitherto associated with the individual mind is now freed and untrammeled and brought into direct contact and unity with the Ultimate Reality. Since there is now no veil between consciousness and the Ultimate Reality, consciousness is fused with the Absolute and eternally abides in It as an inseparable aspect promoting an unending state of infinite knowledge and unlimited bliss...

"God-realisation is a personal state of consciousness belonging to the soul which has transcended the domain of the mind. Other souls continue to remain in bondage and though they also are bound to receive God-realisation one day they can only attain it by freeing their consciousness from the burden of the ego and the limitations of the individual mind. Hence the attainment of God-realisation has a direct significance only for the soul which has emerged out of the time-process . . . It is possible for an aspirant to rise up to the mental sphere of existence through his own unaided efforts, but dropping the mental body amounts to the surrenderance of individual existence: This last and all-important step cannot be taken except through the help of a Perfect Master who is himself God-realised."

R.A. Nicholson in Chapter two, being an essay on the book of the Sufi Master 'Abdu 'I-Karim ibn Ibrahim al-Jili (born in 1365)... not to be confused with another famous Perfect Master Gilani born 200 years earlier... 'The Perfect Man' (Insanu 'I-kamil) of his *Studies in Islamic Mysticism* Cambridge University Press 1921 in which his translation states:

"What do Sufis mean when they speak of the Perfect Man (*al-insanu 'I-kamil*), a phrase which seems first to have been used by the celebrated Ibnu 'I-'Arabi, although the notion underlying it is almost as old as Sufism itself? The question might be answered in different ways, but if we seek a general definition, perhaps we may describe the Perfect

Man as a man who has fully realised his essential oneness with the Divine Being in whose likeness he is made. This experience, enjoyed by prophets and saints and shadowed forth in symbols to others, is the foundation of the Sufi theosophy. Therefore, the class of Perfect Men comprises not only the prophets from Adam to Mohammed, but also the superlatively elect *(khususu 'l-khusus)* amongst the Sufis, i.e., the persons named collectively *awliya,* plural of *wali,* a word originally meaning "near," which is used for "friend," *"protége,"* or "devotee." Since the *wali* or saint is the popular type of Perfect Man, it should be understood that the essence of Mohammedan saintship, as of prophecy, is nothing less than Divine illumination, immediate vision and knowledge of things unseen and unknown, when the veil of sense is suddenly lifted and the conscious self passes away in the overwhelming glory of "the One true Light." An ecstatic feeling of oneness with God constitutes the *wali.* It is the end of the Path *(tariqa)* in so far as the discipline of the Path is meant to predispose and prepare the disciple to receive this incalculable gift of Divine grace, which is not gained or lost by anything that a man may do, but comes to him in proportion to the measure and degree of spiritual capacity with which he was created.

"Two special functions of the *wali* further illustrate the relation of the popular saint-cult to mystical philosophy—(1) his function as a mediator, (2) his function as a cosmic power. The Perfect Man, as will be explained in the course of our argument, unites the One and the Many, so that the universe depends on him for its continued existence. In Mohammedan religious life the *wali* occupies the same middle position: he bridges the chasm which the Koran and scholasticism have set between man and an absolutely transcendent God. He brings relief to the distressed, health to the sick, children to the childless, food to the famished, spiritual guidance to those who entrust their souls to his care, blessing to all who visit his tomb and invoke Allah in his name. The walls, from the highest to the lowest, are arranged in a graduated hierarchy, with the *Qutub* at their head, forming "a saintly board of administration by which the invisible government of the world is carried on." Speaking of the *Awtad*—four saints whose rank is little inferior to that of the *Qutub* himself- Hujwiri (*Kashaf al-Mahjub* of Al-Hujwiri, R.A. Nicholson translation Luzac & Co, London 1911, page 228) says: 'It is their office to go round the whole world every night, and if there be any place on which their eyes have not fallen, next day some flaw will appear in that place; and they must then inform the *Qutub,* in order that he may direct his attention to the weak spot, and that by his blessing the imperfection may be remedied.'

"Such experiences and beliefs were partly the cause and partly the consequence of speculation concerning the nature of God and man, speculation which drifted far away from Koranic monotheism into pantheistic and monistic philosophies. The Sufi reciting the Koran in ecstatic prayer and seeming to hear, in the words which he intoned, not his own voice but the voice of God speaking through him, could no longer acquiesce in the orthodox conception of Allah as a Being utterly different from all other beings. This dogma was supplanted by faith in a Divine Reality (al-Haqq), a God who is the creative principle and ultimate ground of all that exists. While Sufis, like Moslems in general, affirm the transcendence of God and reject the notion of infusion or incarnation (hulul), it is an interesting fact that one of the first attempts in Islam to indicate more precisely the meaning of mystical union was founded on the Christian doctrine of two natures in God. Hallaj, who dared to say *Ana 'l-Haqq,* 'I am the *Haqq,*' thereby announced that the saint in his deification "becomes the living and personal witness of God." The Jewish tradition that God created Adam in His own image reappeared as a *hadith* (saying of the Prophet) and was put to strange uses by Mohammedan theosophists. Even the orthodox Ghazali hints that here is the key of a great mystery which nothing will induce him to divulge. According to Hallaj, the essence of God's essence is Love. Before the creation God loved Himself in absolute unity and through love revealed Himself to Himself alone. Then, desiring to behold that love-in-aloneness, that love without otherness and duality, as an external object, He brought forth from non-existence an image of Himself, endowed with all His attributes and names. This Divine image is Adam, in and by whom God is made manifest--divinity objectified in humanity. Hallaj, however, distinguishes the human nature (nasut) from the Divine (lahut). Though mystically united, they are not essentially identical and interchangeable. Personality survives even in union: water does not become wine, though wine be mixed with it. Using a more congenial metaphor, Hallaj says in verses which are often quoted:

> *I'm the One I love, the One I love is me,*
> *we are two spirits that live... in one body.*
> *If you see me, then... you see that One,*
> *and, if you see that One... both, you see.*

"…Jili belongs to the school of Sufis who hold that Being is one, that all apparent differences are modes, aspects and manifestations of reality, that the phenomenal is the outward expression of the real. He begins by defining essence as that to which names and attributes are referred; it may be either existent or non-existent, *i.e.,* existing only in name, like the fabulous bird called 'Anqa. Essence that really exists is of two kinds: Pure Being, or God, and Being joined to not-being, *i.e.,* the world of created things. The essence of God is unknowable *per se;* we must seek knowledge of it through its names and attributes. It is a substance with two accidents, eternity and everlastingness; with two qualities, creativeness and creatureliness; with two descriptions, uncreatedness and origination in time; with two names, Lord and slave (God and man); with two aspects, the outward or visible, which is the present world, and the inward or invisible, which is the world to come; both necessity and contingency are predicated of it, and it may be regarded either as non-existent for itself but existent for other, or as non-existent for other but existent for itself.

"Pure Being, as such, has neither name nor attribute; only when it gradually descends from its absoluteness and enters the realm of manifestation, do names and attributes appear imprinted on it. The sum, of these attributes is the universe, which is 'phenomenal' only in the sense that it shows reality under the form of externality. Although, from this standpoint, the distinction of essence and attribute must be admitted, the two are ultimately one, like water and ice. The so-called phenomenal world—the world of attributes—is no illusion: it really exists as the self-revelation or other self of the Absolute. In denying any real difference between essence and attribute, Jili makes Being identical with Thought. The world expresses God's idea of Himself, or as Ibnu 'l-'Arabi puts it, 'we ourselves are the attributes by which we describe God; our existence is merely an objectification of His existence. God is necessary to us in order that we may exist, while we are necessary to Him in order that He may be manifested to Himself.'

"Jili calls the simple essence, apart from all qualities and relations, 'the dark mist' *(al-'Ama)*. It develops consciousness by passing through three stages of manifestation, which modify its simplicity. The first stage is Oneness *(Ahadiyya)*, the second is He-ness *(Huwiyya)*, and the third is I-ness *(Aniyya)*. By this process of descent Absolute Being has become the subject and object of all thought and has revealed itself as Divinity with distinctive attributes embracing the whole series of existence. The created world is the outward aspect of that which in its inward aspect is God. Thus in the Absolute we find a principle of diversity, which it evolves by moving downwards, so to speak, from a plane beyond quality and relation, beyond even the barest unity, until by degrees it clothes itself with manifold names and attributes and takes visible shape in the infinite variety of Nature. But 'the One remains, the Many change and pass.' The Absolute cannot rest in diversity. Opposites must be reconciled and at last united, the Many must again be One. Recurring to Jili's metaphor, we may say that as water becomes ice and then water once more, so the Essence crystallised in the world of attributes seeks to return to its pure and simple self. And in order to do so, it must move upwards, reversing the direction of its previous descent from absoluteness. We have seen how reality, without ceasing to be reality, presents itself in the form of appearance: by what means, then, does appearance cease to be appearance and disappear in the abysmal darkness of reality?

"Man, in virtue of his essence, is the cosmic Thought assuming flesh and connecting Absolute Being with the world of Nature.

"While every appearance shows some attribute of reality, Man is the microcosm in which all attributes are united, and in him alone does the Absolute become conscious of itself in all its diverse aspects. To put it in another way, the Absolute, having completely realised itself in human nature, returns into itself through the medium of human nature; or, more intimately, God and man become one in the Perfect Man—the enraptured prophet or saint—whose religious function as a mediator between man and God corresponds with his metaphysical function as the unifying principle by means of which the opposed terms of reality and appearance are harmonised. Hence the upward movement of the Absolute from the sphere of manifestation back to the unmanifested Essence takes place in and through the unitive experience of the soul; and so we have exchanged philosophy for mysticism.

"Jili distinguishes three phases of mystical illumination or revelation (tajalli), which run parallel, as it were, to the three stages—Oneness, He-ness, and I-ness—traversed by the Absolute in its descent to consciousness.

"In the first phase, called the Illumination of the Names, the Perfect Man receives the mystery that is conveyed by each of the names of

God, and he becomes one with the name in such sort that he answers the prayer of any person who invokes God by the name in question.

"Similarly, in the second phase he receives the Illumination of the Attributes and becomes one with them, *i.e.,* with the Divine Essence as qualified by its various attributes: life, knowledge, power, will, and so forth. For example, God reveals Himself to some mystics through the attribute of life. Such a man, says Jili, is the life of, the whole universe; he feels that his life permeates all things sensible and ideal, that all words, deeds, bodies, and spirits derive their existence from him. If he be endued with the attribute of knowledge, he knows the entire content of past, present, and future existence, how everything came to be or is coming or will come to be, and why the non-existent does not exist: all this he knows both synthetically and analytically. The Divine attributes are classified by the author under four heads: (1) attributes of the Essence, (2) attributes of Beauty, (3) attributes of Majesty, (4) attributes of Perfection. He says that all created things are mirrors in which Absolute Beauty is reflected. What is ugly has its due place in the order of existence no less than what is beautiful, and equally belongs to the Divine perfection: evil, therefore, is only relative. As was stated above, the Perfect Man reflects all the Divine attributes, including even the Essential ones, such as unity and eternity, which he shares with no other being in this world or the next.

"The third and last phase is the Illumination of the Essence. Here the Perfect Man becomes *absolutely* perfect. Every attribute has vanished, the Absolute has returned into itself.

27

"In the theory thus outlined we can recognise a monistic form of the myth which represents the Primal Man, the first-born of God, as sinking into matter, working there as a creative principle, longing for deliverance, and, at last finding the way back to his source. Jili calls the Perfect Man the preserver of the universe, the *Qutb* or Pole on which all the spheres of existence revolve. He is the final cause of creation, *i.e.*, the means by which God sees Himself, for the Divine names and attributes cannot be seen, as a whole, except in the Perfect Man. He is a copy made in the image of God; therefore in him is that which corresponds to the Essence with its two correlated aspects of He-ness and I-ness, *i.e.*, inwardness and outwardness, or divinity and humanity. His real nature is threefold, as Jili expressly declares in the following verses, which no one can read without wondering how a Moslem could have written them:

If you say that it (the Essence) is One, you are right;

or if you say that it is Two, it is in fact Two.

Or if you say, 'No, it is Three,' you are right,

for that is the real nature of Man." (End of Nicholson quote)

The Tomb of Hallaj in Karkh.

'Anal-Haqq' or 'I am the Truth' of Hallaj.

In his book of 'lectures' *The Idea of Personality in Sufism* the great translator of Rumi's work and other Sufi poets R.A. Nicholson states... "The words *Ana 'l-Haqq* occur in an extraordinary book composed by Hallaj, the *Kitab al-Tawasin,* which was edited in 1913 by M. Louis Massignon. Written in rhymed Arabic prose and divided into eleven brief sections, it sets forth a doctrine of saintship—a doctrine founded on personal experience and clothed in the form of a subtle yet passionate dialectic. The style is so technical and obscure that even with the help of the Persian commentary we can sometimes only guess what meaning the writer intended to convey. Instead of translating the text, the editor has devoted years of patient labour to understanding and illustrating it, with the result that his monograph on Hallaj must be studied carefully by everyone interested in Sufism. For it is now clear that the words *Ana l'-Haqq* were not the ejaculation of visionary enthusiasm but the intuitive formula in which a whole system of mystical theology summed itself up. And this system is not only the first in time, it is also profoundly original. The power and vitality of this man's ideas are attested by the influence which they asserted upon his successors. His ashes were scattered, swept away, as he prophesied, by rushing winds and running waters, but his words lived after him and we see them, all through the Middle Ages, rising like sparks and kindling to new life.

I cannot attempt to give you a full account of the doctrines contained in the *Tasawin* and supplemented by numerous fragments which Massignon has collected. We may begin by asking, "What did Hallaj mean when he said *Ana 'l-Haqq?*" The expression *al-Haqq* is commonly used by Sufis to denote the Creator as opposed to *al-khalq*, "the creatures," and there is no doubt that it bears this signification here: *Ana 'l-Haqq.* "I am the Creative Truth," as Massignon renders it (*Tawasin,* p.175).

"Hallaj," he says, "while affirming the transcendence of the idea of God, did not at all conceive it as being inaccessible to man. From the old Jewish and Christian tradition that God created man in His own image Hallaj deduced a doctrine of creation, which had its counterpart in a doctrine of deification: the deified man finds in himself, by means of 9a mystical) asceticism, the reality of the Divine image which God has imprinted on him. We possess several Hallajian fragments that leave no doubt as to this. In the longest, Hallaj explains the matter thus: Before all things, before the creation, before His knowledge of the creation, God in His unity was holding an ineffable discourse with Himself and contemplating the splendour of His essence in itself. That pure simplicity of His self-admiration is Love, which in His essence is the essence of the essence, beyond all limitation of attributes. In His perfect isolation God loves Himself, praises Himself, and manifests Himself by Love. And it was this first manifestation of Love in the Divine Absolute that determined the multiplicity of His attributes and His names. Then God, by His essence, in His essence, desired to project out of Himself his supreme joy, that Love in its aloneness, that He might behold it and speak to it. He looked in eternity and brought forth from non-existence and image, an image of Himself, endowed with all His attributes and all His names: Adam. The Divine look made that form to be His image unto everlasting. God saluted it, glorified it, chose it, and inasmuch as He manifested Himself by it and in it, that created form became *Huwa Huwa,* He, He!" (*Tawasin* page 129).

The first of the following verses by Hallaj refers to Adam, the second is said to refer to Jesus:

Glory to God Who revealed in His humanity the secret of His radiant divinity.

And then appeared to His creatures visibly in the shape of one who eats and drinks. (Tawasin p. 130)

Here you will notice, we have the doctrine of two natures in God—a divine nature *(lahut)* and a human nature *(nasut).* These terms are borrowed by Syrian Christianity, which uses them to denote the two natures of Christ. Further, Hallaj in describing the union of the *lahut* with the *nasut*—or, as he generally says, of the Divine Spirit with the human spirit—employs the term *hulul;* and *hulul* is a word associated, in Muslim minds, with the Christian doctrine of the Incarnation. In his poems his own spirit and the Divine Spirit appear as lovers conversing with each other and most intimately united.

Thy Spirit is mingled in my spirit even as wine is mingled in pure water.

When everything touches Thee, it touches me. Lo, in every case Thou art I. (Tawasin p.134)

And again:

I am He whom I love, and He whom I love is I,
We are two spirits dwelling in one body.
If thou seest me, thou seest Him.

And if thou seest Him, thou seest us both.

(Tawasin p. 134)

While Hallaj asserts the pre-existence of Mohammad as the Light from which all prophecy emanates, it is not Mohammad but Jesus in whom he finds the perfect type of the 'deified man', whose personality is not destroyed but transfigured and essentialised, so that he stands forth as the personal witness and representative of God, revealing from within himself *al-Haqq*, the Creator through whom he exists, the Creative Truth in whom he has all his being. (*Tawasin* pp 162, 175.) End of quote of Nicholson.

In his great *masnavi* poem that has become a famous manual of Sufism 'The Rose Garden of Mysteries' the Sufi Master Poet Shabistari (1250-1320) commenting on this saying of Hallaj poses the following question...

QUESTION

'I am The Truth!' When, to reveal this is appropriate?
Why call that one a babbler... vain imposter, incarnate?

ANSWER

'I am The Truth' is a revelation of absolute mystery,
and... except for 'The Truth' who revealing it can be?
All of the atoms of the world, all of those like Mansur,
one could think to be drunk and heavy with wine, for
they are continually singing this song full of praise...
they in this spiritual truth are spending all their days.

If you desire that its meaning be made clear to you,

then go and be reading the text 'God, all praise You'.

When eventually the 'self' as cotton you have carded,

from you like that 'wool-carder' such will be shouted.

Take out from your ears that cotton of your illusion…

be listening to the call of… 'The Almighty, the One'.

From 'The Truth' this call is always coming to you…

so why are you waiting for the last day… to be true?

Come into the 'valley of peace' because immediately

the bush will be saying to you 'Truly I am God', see?

If 'I am The Truth' for the burning bush was lawful,

why… in mouth of a good man would it be unlawful?

Every one whose heart is purified, without any doubt,

that exists no being but One, knows without a doubt.

To be saying 'I am', only to 'The Truth' is belonging,

for both essence and illusory appearance is not being.

Glory of 'The Truth' does not allow for any duality…

because there is no 'I' or 'We' or 'You' in that Glory!

'I' and 'We' and 'You' and 'He' are all only one thing,

because in Unity there is no distinction of and being.

And so, every person who as a void is of self empty,

in that one is echoing 'I am The Truth'… constantly;

that one is taking his side that is eternal, 'other' dies,

the traveler and travel and traveling… all in One lies.

From the 'other' incarnation, communion are springing,

but… from the spiritual journey the Unity is arriving.

Separated from 'The Truth' is illusionary existence...

'The Truth' is no creature; God, none does experience.

Here... Incarnation and Communion are impossible;

because, duality within unity is obviously impossible.

The existence of creatures and diversity is an illusion,

for not all that seems to be can honestly be relied upon.

(From, 'The Rose Garden of Mysteries' by Shabistari, Translation & Introduction by Paul Smith, New Humanity Books, Campbells Creek, 2012.

Four Master Poets of Baghdad who influenced Hallaj.

AL NURI (d.907). Abu 'l-Husayn al-Nuri was a native of Baghdad. He was a friend of al-Junaid who was for a time the Spiritual Master of Hallaj. He was a leading figure of Sufism in the region. His name 'Nuri' means 'Man of Light.'

Al-Nuri was devout and had an ascetic temperament. It is said that when he left for work in the morning, he would buy a few loaves of bread and then distribute them to the poor on his walk. He would then go to the mosque and pray until noon before arriving at work... never having eaten food for himself.

But even with his compassion and his striving, at a certain point he became frustrated that he was still buffeted with desires and hadn't penetrated to inner mystical truth. He then made a firm resolve to follow God's will in everything and not to be distracted by comforts and desires. He was determined to confront every aspect of himself, even considering the possibility that his past striving and good works had been hypocritical... a determination to remove all falsity and barriers between himself and God.

In this process, he began to recognize that the carnal mind, the grasping, false self, claimed a portion of everything the heart touched. Thus, when God sent him divine insight, this grasping identity stole a portion of it... which explained the poverty of his mystical experience to that point. From that point on, he thwarted the false self at every turn. Even in service to others, if he found the carnal mind gaining satisfaction, he quickly stopped and sought new ways to help others.

Al-Nuri said that through doing this he slowly discovered the way to true mystical insight.

Further Reading...

Anthology of Classical Arabic Poetry, Translation & Introduction by Paul Smith, New Humanity Books, Campbells Creek, 2009.
Sufi Poems, A Medieval Anthology by Martin Lings, Islamic Texts Society, Cambridge, 2004. (Pages 16-19).
A Critical Appreciation of Arabic Mystical Poetry by Dr. S.H. Nadeem, Adam Publishers. New Delhi, 2003.
The Way of the Mystics: The Early Christian Mystics and the Rise of the Sufis by Margaret Smith... reprint Sheldon Press 1976.
In the Garden of Myrtles: Studies in Early Islamic Mysticism by Tor Andrae, Translated by Birgitta Sharpe. State University of New York Press, Albany. 1987.
Muslim Saints and Mystics... Episodes from the Tadhkirat al-Auliya' (The Lives of the Saints) by Farid al-Din 'Attar Translated by A.J. Arberry. Routledge & Kegan Paul 1966. (Pages 221-231.)

Some examples of his poetry...

Qit'as...

"Don't tell," You said, then... into mysteries beyond any speech

You took my questioning soul: can any words describe the

indescribable?

Not each one who cries, "Look, I am this," one takes his word:

when deeds show one is so then You him as Your own find

claimable.

Through concentration, 'I' would go, a path to You, I'd set:
but, none may come to You, except, as You want them to.
Lord I can't without You, but Your hand stops me leaving:
some desired to come to You... this hope You created, too;
see, I've cut off all thought... killed me, so I'm only Yours:
heart's Beloved, how long? With separation... I'm through.

"For tomorrow's festival," they cried, "what robe will you wear?"
I replied: "Robe He gave, Who poured me many a bitter potion:
poverty, patience cover a heart seeing at every feast its Lover...
can there be finer garb to greet Friend than one He lends to one?
When You aren't near, each moment is an age of grief, and fear:
if I see and hear You, days are joyful, life's a festival in the sun!"

God, I fear You: not because I dread any wrath to come:
how can one fear... You are the best Friend, obviously?
You know my heart's design, the mind's secret purpose:
I adore You, Divine Light, a lesser light would blind me.

I'm veiled from Time and my veil's my feeling for Him:
this wonder in me for His Infinite value... more than I!
Time cannot see that I have slipped through its hands...
and I do not see Time's works anymore, or how they fly,
because I am now only awake to be fulfilling His order,
and the rest of my life for Time why should I care... why?

My love overflows such that I'd remember Him forever;

and yet my remembering, that'd be amazing to explain,

has become ecstasy; and it is amazing that even ecstasy

from any memory of near and far, has vanished... again!

*

JUNAID (830-910). Junaid ibn Muhammad Abu al-Qasim al-Khazzaz al-Baghdadi was one of the great early Sufis.

He laid the groundwork for *sober* mysticism in contrast to that of *God-intoxicated* Sufis like Bayazid Bistami, Mansur Hallaj and Abu Said. In the process of the trial of Hallaj his former disciple, the caliph of the time demanded his death and he issued this: "From the outward appearance he is to die and we judge according to the outward appearance and God knows better."

Further Reading...

The Life, Personality and Writings of Al-Junayd. Edited and Translated by Dr. Ali Hassan Abdel-Kader, Luzac, 1978.
A Critical Appreciation of Arabic Mystical Poetry by Dr. S.H. Nadeem, Adam Publishers. New Delhi, 2003.
The Way of the Mystics: The Early Christian Mystics and the Rise of the Sufis by Margaret Smith... reprint Sheldon Press 1976.
In the Garden of Myrtles: Studies in Early Islamic Mysticism by Tor Andrae, Translated by Birgitta Sharpe. State University of New York Press, Albany. 1987.
Muslim Saints and Mystics... Episodes from the Tadhkirat al-Auliya' (The Lives of the Saints) by Farid al-Din 'Attar Translated by A.J. Arberry. Routledge & Kegan Paul 1966. (pages 192-214.)
Anthology of Classical Arabic Poetry, Translation & Introduction by Paul Smith, New Humanity Books, Campbells Creek, 2009.

Some examples of his poetry…

Qit'as…

Over their hearts flew His desire and they arrived

in the neighbourhood of that perfect, glorified One.

Under His glory's shadow they are close to Him,

there where their souls are stirring under His Sun.

They're going there to discover honour and insight

and they're returning with every kind of perfection.

They march with the unique glory of that One's

attributes and they're trailing robes of Unification.

And what happens next is far beyond any way of

describing, so, it is best let it stay a secret, my son.

You, burner of my heart's fire with Your omnipotence,

if You'd wanted You'd have put it out with… Yourself.

If I should die from fear and worry, I won't be blamed

for what You've done to me: it is not because of myself.

O Lord, now I've known what's inside my heart:

secretly, with my Beloved I've held conversation.

And so, in a fashion, we are One, we are united,

but our condition in another is one of separation.

Although awe has hidden You from my glances,

ecstasy brought You into my innermost location.

O God, my God, if You should happen to turn

coldon me… and turn Your face from me away,

my soul could never escape its longing for You,

even if this life it will leave behind… give away.

*

SUMNUN (d. 915). Abu'l-Hasan Sumnun ibn Mamzah al-Basri was from Baghdad and like al-Nuri was a friend of Junaid. He was called *al-Muhibb*, the Lover.

Further Reading…

Sufi Poems, A Medieval Anthology by Martin Lings, Islamic Texts Society, Cambridge, 2004. [Pages 21-25].
Anthology of Classical Arabic Poetry, Translation & Introduction by Paul Smith, New Humanity Books, Campbells Creek, 2009.

Some of his poetry…

Qit'as…

I'm longing at every dawn and as night is falling,

and I answer that one when love calls at night…

as day disappears my love is growing stronger,

although that time of love is now lost from sight.

Inside of me I felt empty, until I discovered Your love:

on life, things, I'd muse slightly, but usually playing;

then, when my heart was called by Your love, it went,
and now lost to me forever, it's in Your court, staying.
If I'm lying may separation from You be my payment,
if in the world any joy in other than You I am finding,
and if anything should seem lovely to me in any land,
if to these two eyes of mine... You they're not seeing!
And so, if it's Your will, then bring me to You, or not:
whatever happens, but my heart only You, is wanting!

There's no doubt in my heart You're the Beloved:
it would no longer live again, if this soul lost You.
You made me thirst for Union that You can give
if in You I rested, if "O my thirst!" I cried to You.

Existence of the seer is obliterated by What is seen:
existence is obliterated by It, so it's without meaning.
You tossed me into Your Divinity's ocean, to swim,
where I don't exist but from in You, You I'm desiring.

If once my eye wept or kept watch for other than You,
let it never receive that Gift... that it was longing for!
If it on purpose looked on other than You may it never
graze Faith's meadow, or see Your fair face, anymore.

SHIBLI (861-946). A pupil and disciple of Junaid of Baghdad and one who had met and was a friend of... Mansur Hallaj, Shibli is one of the famous Sufis. He was originally from Khurasan. In the book *Rawdat al-jannat,* and in other biographies, many mystical poems and sayings have been recorded of him. Ansari has said: "The first person to speak in symbols was Dhu al-Nun of Egypt. Then came Junaid and he systematized this science, extended it, and wrote books on it. Shibli, in his turn, took it to the pulpit." He died in 946 at the age of 87. He composed his poems in Arabic.

Further Reading...

A Critical Appreciation of Arabic Mystical Poetry by Dr. S.H. Nadeem, Adam Publishers. New Delhi, 2003.
Sufi Poems, A Mediaeval Anthology by Martin Lings, Islamic Texts Society, Cambridge, 2004 (Pages 41-7).
Muslim Saints and Mystics... Episodes from the Tadhkirat al-Auliya' (The Lives of the Saints) by Farid al-Din 'Attar Translated by A.J. Arberry. Routledge & Kegan Paul 1966. (Pages 277-287.)
Anthology of Classical Arabic Poetry, Translation & Introduction by Paul Smith, New Humanity Books, Campbells Creek, 2009.

Some of his poems...

Ruba'i...

I will put upon me a fine robe of patience...

keeping awake at night for longer makes sense.

I am not yet willing to be patient completely...

a bit at a time soul I'll try bring, to my defence.

Qit'as...

The science of the Sufis has no bound,
a science, high, celestial and divine...
in it, hearts of Masters' plunged deep;
men of wisdom know them by that sign.

Majnun declared his love, while I concealed
my passion... so I attained ecstasy's state.
On the Day of Judgement, when lovers are
called to come up... only I will as a lover rate!

A friend asked, "How's Your patience with them?"
I replied, "Does patience exist? I need to be asked?"
The heat of love in my heart is more fierce than fire,
more sweet than piety...sharper than a knife whetted.

I mentioned You, not because I'd forgotten You, even
momentarily... to remember with the tongue is easier.
From ecstasy I'd almost died... such was my longing,
and I was so anxious my heart kept beating... faster!
Then, when the ecstasy revealed to me You were here
before me... I then did see Your presence, everywhere!
So I communicated with the Existence without words
and saw One I knew, without having to at One stare.

Glancing my way He let me see how much He cared:
I was aflame, it melted my heart, as He moved away.
He isn't *not* here, as consolation I can remember Him,
and He never *really* left… and now 'I' might go away!

This case of mine is strange, I'm unique in this state:
among mankind I'm the only one: none, is beyond me!
I am eternally in Your form and 'me', You obliterated:
so, I am not now of created beings… in fact, I'm Free!

Surely you'll have heard that I was staying
in saints' brotherhood, under poets' cupola?
Truth was, I was afraid of being with both,
so with poetry and song I acted like another
with crazy acts of joy or agony and allowed
myself to be placed in a hospital to recover!
I feared of being alone with One, Beloved…
I feared death, old or young, like some other.
That is why I threw a rose as he was on the
cross performing an ablution in blood there.
Mine were acts of a mad lover, it saved me:
bringing death… his out of his reason were.

A Selection of Poetry from the Persian, Turkish & Pushtu poets about or influenced by Mansur Hallaj.

(Note: All of the poems below are couplets from longer poems in the forms of the *ghazal, qi'ta, masnavi, qasida*)

ABU SA'ID (968-1049) was a Perfect Master and a poet who lived in Nishapur and composed only *ruba'is,* over 400 of them. He was one of the founders of Persian Sufi and Dervish poetry and a major influence on the *ruba'i* and most poets that followed, especially Sana'i, Nizami, 'Attar and Rumi.

Translation from...

Ruba'iyat of Abu Sa'id. Translation & Introduction by Paul Smith, New Humanity Books, Campbells Creek 2010.

> Mansur Hallaj, a crocodile in Unification's
>
> river...
>
> effaced himself and with the Absolute was a
>
> uniter.
>
> "I'm the Absolute Truth," one day he was declaring:
>
> so where was the Almighty One and where
>
> Mansur?

*

ANSARI (1005-1090). The great mystical poet Khwaja Abdullah Ansari who passed from this world 1089 in Herat is most famous for his biographical dictionary on saints and Sufi masters and his much loved collection of inspiring prayers, the *Munajat.* His *ruba'is* appear throughout his works.

Translation from…

Ansari: Selected Poems, Translation & Introduction by Paul Smith, New Humanity Books, Campbells Creek, 2008.
Ruba'iyat of Ansari, Translation & Introduction by Paul Smith, New Humanity Books, Campbells Creek, 2009.

"I am God," Hallaj said and the gibbet

crowned:

"God," Abdullah exclaimed, was met...

crowned.

I have also said what was said by Hallaj:

Hallaj said it out loud, I inside, yet…

crowned!

*

MU'IN (1141-1230) Muhammad Mu'inuddin Chishti was also known as *Gharib Nawaz* or 'Benefactor of the Poor', he is the most famous Sufi saint and poet of the Chishti Order of the Indian Subcontinent. He introduced and established the order in South Asia. The initial spiritual chain of the Chishti order in India, comprising himself, Bakhtiyar Kaki, Baba Farid and Nizamuddin Auliya (each successive person being the disciple of the previous one), constitutes the great Sufi saints of Indian history.

Translation from…

Mu'in ud-din Chishti: Selected Poems, Translation & Introduction by Paul

It wasn't only Mansur who was drunk on love's wine,

the scaffold to the rope the same tale was telling...

"It is all that One!"

The heart freely tells the secret of love and isn't afraid,

as it knows that in what is seen and what's hiding.

it is all that One!

Lift veil of dust and water from off the face of heart and soul,

so that all the darkness of your existence into the light is

turning.

Whoever drinks cup of Eternity in this assembly of existence

holds the rope of Union with God... and the scaffold is

ascending.

If with the eyes of the lover You could see Your beauty...

like me You'd be thinking of only You... night and

day!

Mu'in desires the wine that will take him from himself,

so like Mansur he will unite with You... straight

away.

A drop from Love's ocean was source of Mansur's state:

anything else into the lover's cup to be tasted,

is what?

O Mu'in, if with tongue you speak of God's mysteries...

such a one's place is not a pulpit... the gibbet

is what!

From the cup of Union with God give me a drink,

so in this passing world another Mansur

I am.

Give me from cup which secret of 'I am God' may

come from my tongue and excused forever

I am.

*

'ATTAR (d. 1230). Farid al-din 'Attar is the Perfect Master Poet who was the author of over forty books of poetry and prose including *The Conference of the Birds, The Book of God,* and *The Lives of the Saints.* Apart from his many books in *masnavi* form he also composed many hundreds of mystical *ghazals* and *ruba'is.* He also changed the evolution of the *ruba'i* form by composing a long Sufi epic, the *Mukhtar-nama,* where each *ruba'i* is connected to the one before, something which Fitzgerald attempted to do with those he attributed to Omar Khayyam over six hundred years later.

He was killed by the Mongol invaders outside the gates of Nishapur when at over a hundred years old he advanced on them alone, sword in hand. It is said that after his head was cut off he kept on fighting. In his masterpiece long *masnavi poem Ilahi-nama,* 'Book of God, that was to influence Jalal-al-Din Rumi in the composing of his six book masterpiece *Masnavi*.

Translation from...

Ruba'iyat of 'Attar. Translation & Introduction by Paul Smith, New Humanity Books, Campbells Creek, 2009.
'Attar: Selected Poetry. Translation, Introduction & Notes by Paul Smith, New Humanity Books, Campbells Creek, 2010.

If you want to know Love's mystery give up faith

and infidelity: Love comes and makes both, expire.

Thousands of travellers on Love's road lay claim:

in this circle of the way, Hallaj is the gem on fire.

It is a difficult and great task, this mystical path...

thousand travellers, but just one sees Path, entire.

*

RUMI (1207-1273). Jalal-ud-din Rumi was born in Balkh. He moved when about eleven with his family away from Balkh so as to avoid the warlike Mongols. They travelled to Baghdad, to Mecca on pilgrimage, to Damascus and eventually settled near Konya in what is now western Turkey.

On the road to Anatolia, Jalal-ud-din and his father had encountered one of the most famous mystic Persian poets, Farid al-din 'Attar, in the city of Nishapur. 'Attar immediately recognized the boy's spiritual status.

For nine years, Rumi practiced Sufism as a disciple of his father Burhan-ud-din until his father died in 1240. During this period Rumi travelled to Damascus and is said to have spent four years there. While there he first caught a glimpse of the *Qutub* (Perfect Master) Shams-e Tabriz. Rumi's love and his great longing for Shams found expression in music, dance, songs and poems in his collection of poems/songs or *Divan* which he named after his Master... *Divan of Shams-e Tabriz.* This vast work included thousands of *ghazals* and other poetic forms and nearly two thousand *ruba'is* that he would compose for many years, before he became a God-realized Perfect Master. Rumi's disciple Hesam'odin Hasan urged Rumi to write the *'Masnavi'* in the style of Sana'i and 'Attar. Rumi completed six books (35,000 couplets) of these before he died.

Translation from...

Rumi: Selected Poems, Translation & Introduction by Paul Smith, New Humanity Books, Campbells Creek, 2009.

Every true lover is likened to Mansur, in that they killed themselves:

reveal any one but a lover, who deliberately, himself is exterminating!

A hundred requisitions are made by Death every day upon mankind...

the lover of God, without asking for anything... himself, is slaying.

One who gets mixed up in Your Love for even a

moment

will experience personal disaster to an incredible

extent.

When Mansur Hallaj revealed Love's Secret...

he was hung by the throat of rope of that zealous

establishment.

It is a party... do not be here without

tambourine...

get up, the drum beat, we're Mansur

obviously.

We're intoxicated, but not from wine:

we're far from anything you thought to

be!

Wool-carder Hallaj, who... " I am the Truth," declared;

swept God's dust from each road, on which he stepped.

And... when that one in the sea of non-existence dived,

he won for us Pearl when he... "I am the Truth," said.

*

YUNUS EMRE (d. 1321). Yunus Emre is considered by many to be one of the most important Turkish poets excising a great influence on Turkish literature from his own time until the present. He is one of the first known poets to have composed in Turkish of his own age and region rather than in Persian or Arabic, his diction remains very close to the popular speech of his contemporaries in Central and Western Anatolia. Little can be said for certain of his life other than that he was a Sufi dervish of Anatolia. His poetry expresses a deep personal mysticism and humanism and love for God.

He was a contemporary of Rumi, who lived in the same region. Rumi composed his collection of stories and songs for a well-educated urban circle of Sufis, writing primarily in the literary language of Persian. Yunus Emre, on the other hand, traveled and taught among the rural poor, singing his songs in the Turkish language of the common people. A story is told of a meeting between the two great souls: Rumi asked Yunus Emre what he thought of his great work the *Masnavi*. Yunus Emre said, "Excellent, excellent! But I would have done it differently." Surprised, Rumi asked how. Yunus replied, "I would have written, 'I came from the eternal, clothed myself in flesh, and took the name Yunus.'" That story perfectly illustrates Yunus Emre's simple, direct approach that has made him so beloved. Interestingly, the name Yunus means 'dolphin' in Turkish.

Translations from...

Yunus Emre: Selected Poems, Translation & Introduction by Paul Smith, New Humanity Books, Campbells Creek, 2010.

> Before time began I was Mansur, that's the reason I'm here:
> toss my ashes into the sky, 'Ana'l-Hakk' they'll be spelling,
> brother.
> Not burnt though fire burns, not chocked but noose hangs...
> I go where my work's done: I'm here on just a quick outing,
> brother.

For Abraham I made the fire of Nimrod into a vineyard:

disbelief appeared… one who again fire was lighting

is Me!

It was I who said with Hallaj, "I am the living Truth!"

That one who the rope around his neck was placing,

is Me.

When Mustafa, God's beloved, started on the Ascent…

my soul I humbled then and His mystery perceiving,

is Me.

My name is now Yunus at another time it was Isma'il…

for the Beloved, to be a sacrifice, Ararat ascending,

is Me.

Take me to the gallows like Mansur, show me You clearly:

let me sacrifice soul, let me not deny love, let me Love

know.

For agony the remedy is Love, my life I gave up for Love…

Yunus Emre says, "Not for a moment, let me Love

forego!"

Here, those who continually burn are transformed into Light:

that fire is not like any other… there are no flames, not one

sign.

All drunk at that One's gathering sing… "I am the Truth"

like a hundred Hallaj Mansurs: lowest as mad, one could

define.

IBN YAMIN (1286-1368) Amir Fakhr al-Din Mahmud, or Ibn Yamin, was born in Turkistan. His father was a successful poet who taught him the craft and when he died in 1322 left his son wealthy and the role of the court-poet in Khurasan. Ibn Yamin was taken captive when war broke out in 1342 and his royal patron was defeated and his complete *Divan* of poems was destroyed or lost (see the first of the *qit'as* below). Thankfully we still have some of his somewhat cynical *ruba'is*. During the last 25 years of his life he composed a further 5000 couplets.

Translation from…

The Wisdom of Ibn Yamin: Selected Poems, Translation & Introduction by Paul Smith, New Humanity Books, 2011.

> If a palace with nine gilded porches is your desire,
>
> from five senses, four elements, let it be said:
>
> "Depart!"
>
> You'll find no resting place in the abode of pride:
>
> from the gibbet like some Mansur, tortured,
>
> depart.
>
> A snake's no friend for some rich stone inside it:
>
> uproot your greed and from the snake's head
>
> depart!

HAFIZ (1320-1392). Persia's greatest exponent of the *ghazal* and many believe the greatest poet of all time. Shams-ud-din Mohammed (Hafiz), ugly and small, became a God-Realized Perfect Master *(Qutub)*, was twice exiled from his beloved Shiraz for his criticism of rulers and false Sufi masters (such as Shaikh Ali Kolah) and the hypocritical clergy. He was by far the greatest influence on the poets of his time including Obeyd Zakani (possibly his former teacher). His most gifted student, Jahan Khatun (to follow), composed many *ghazals* based on his and praised him in a number of them.

He has been one of the greatest influences in every way on poets, mystics, philosophers and artists in both the East and West. (See my chapter on 'Hafiz's Influence on the East and the West' in my *Divan of Hafiz*).

His *Divan* shows he composed in other forms other than the *ghazal* that he perfected... including his famous *masnavis* 'Book of the Winebringer' and 'Book of the Minstrel' and 'The Wild Deer'... as well as *ruba'is* of which about 150 have come down to us. As with his immortal *ghazals*, his *ruba'is* are sometimes mystical and sometimes critical of the hypocrisy of his times. Apart from *ruba'is* and *ghazals* he composed his masterpiece *masnavis*, *qit'as*, *qasidas* and a quite wonderful and unique *mukhammas*.

Translations from...

Divan of Hafiz: Translation & Introduction by Paul Smith New Humanity Books 1986. New Humanity Books 2006

At the Beginning, love and drunkenness seemed O so easy...

but in the end the soul tired and worn out from the chase is.

This subtlety, sweet singing Hallaj sang before decapitation:

"To question theologians now, the wrong time and place is."

I have given my heart to a Friend, fair and bold and delicate,

Who having an agreeable disposition, such pure grace has.

Those on gallows like Mansur obtain desired remedy:

those delving into thinking of a remedy, find pain too

distressing.

When those longing beg in that Presence, grace comes to

this Court They call Hafiz, when, They cause him to be

dying.

My blood will write 'I am The Truth' [Anal Haq] on the earth,

if like Mansur they kill me on the gallows, mercilessly, tonight.

Beloved, You possess Divine Wealth, I'm beggar at Your door,

give the gift of Your Glory, make me blissfully happy tonight.

All the time I'm frightened that Hafiz will be lost, obliterated;

for every moment I am in possession of such ecstasy, tonight.

JAHAN KHATUN (1326-1416?) Daughter of the king of one of Shiraz's most turbulent times... Masud Shah; pupil and lifelong friend of the world's greatest mystical, lyric poet, Hafiz; the object of crazed desire by (among others) Iran's greatest satirist, the outrageous and visionary dervish poet Obeyd Zakani; lover, then wife of womanizer Amin al-Din, a minister of one of Persia's most loved, debauched and tragic rulers... Abu Ishak; imprisoned for twenty years under the Muzaffarids while her young daughter Soltan Bakht mysteriously died, possibly murdered. She was open-minded and scandalous and one of Iran's first feminists... this beautiful and sensuous, petite princess abdicated her royalty twice. She called herself 'a dervish maid' and is one of Iran's greatest poets whose *Divan* is four times larger than Hafiz's and contains 2000 *ghazals* and hundreds of *ruba'is* and *qita's* and a masterpiece *tarji-band* other forms of poetry.

Translations from...

Hafiz's Friend, Jahan Khatun: Persia's Princess Dervish Poet. A Selection of Poems from Her Divan. Translation Paul Smith and Rezvaneh Pashai. New Humanity Books 2006.

My dearest beloved, those wagging tongues told
you to stay away from your lover who's in decline.
Even if they want to execute you do not complain...
your thoughts and your actions to Mansur incline.

O breeze, when in the gardens please tell to my beloved,

"You are all that I desire… come, you to unification

take."

I'm joyful for my beloved comes, so tell my rival, "Leave!"

I will talk of beloved, or me like Mansur for execution

take.

*

NESIMI (1369-1417). Seyyid Ali Imadaddin Nesimi is considered one of the greatest mystical poets of the late 14th and early 15th centuries and one of the most prominent early masters in Turkish literary history.

Very little is known for certain about his life, including his real name. It is also possible that he was descended from the Prophet Mohammed since he has sometimes been accorded the title of *seyyid* that is reserved for people claimed to be in Muhammad's line of descent. Nesimi's birthplace, like his real name, is wrapped in mystery: some claim that he was born in a province called Nesim, hence the pen-name. According to the Encyclopedia of Islam Nesimi was proficient also in Arabic and Persian and composed poems in both.

From his poetry, it's evident that Nesimi was greatly influenced by Mansur Hallaj and as a direct result of his beliefs that were considered blasphemous by contemporary religious authorities he was seized and according to most accounts… skinned alive in Aleppo.

A number of legends later grew up around his execution, such as the story that he mocked his executioners with improvised verse and, after the execution, draped his flayed skin around his shoulders and departed.

His tomb in Aleppo remains an important place of pilgrimage to this day.

His work consists of two collections of poems, one of which, the rarer, is in Persian and the other in Turkish. The Turkish *Divan* consists of 250-300 *ghazals* and about 150 *ruba'is*. After his death his work continued to exercise a great influence on many Turkish language poets and authors.

Translations from…

Nesimi: Selected Poems, Translation & Introduction by Paul Smith, New Humanity Books, Campbells Creek, 2009.

"I am the Truth!" I cry, for like Mansur, the Truth helped
me!
I was this city's fortress so who wanted to on gibbet, me,
see?
I'm the Shrine of all that is true, the Beloved of the loving devotees…
I'm Mansur of the worthy few and the heavenly *Kaaba*…
truthfully.

One drunk on Love in this world says, "I… am God!"
Mansur Hallaj is soon going to be hanging…
in intoxicated bliss.
This heart is manifested Light, Mt Sanai… our body:
our soul is like Moses that one can be seeing,
in intoxicated bliss.

If I should as Mansur once did, state: "I am God!"

Sir, I'm blameless, gallows taking breath away

I've found!

If you are fascinated like Moses by the face of God,

see yourself inside yourself and then this say:

"I've found!"

For that one's curls infamy Nesimi gave up fidelity:

you in dervish-coat, Christian hair-belt today

I've found!

Your form says, "I'm God!" I'll hang in Your curls noose.

One hung like Mansur, from love's noose isn't returning.

Show things of hypocrites are rosaries and prayer-mats...

Your perfumed curls shall into belts for Your, be turning.

O lover, if today with your Beloved you should be united

come here: like Nesimi this world with a kick be rejecting.

If for saying, "I am God" I'm hung, why should I be grieving?

Upon the gallows was not Mansur hung for all to see?

Come, see!

My heart's cut into pieces from grief due to parting from You:

Beloved, from my eye-wounds blood flows profusely...

come, see!

On this earth it's only the drunkards who leave a mark:

yes, Mansur was right... all life is lit up by love's spark.

O heart, the Truth... it lies in you, the Truth

is in you!

State the Truth, because: "I am the Truth...

is in you!

The Absolute Essence, the Absolute Truth

is in you!

Writing of the Book, by all true... in Truth,

is in you!

*

JAMI (Nov. 7, 1414- Nov. 9, 1492). Considered the last great poet of
the Classical Period (9th-15th c.) Mulla Nur al-Din 'Abd al-Rahman
ibn Ahmad Jami composed forty-three books but is mostly known for his
seven *masnavis* epics greatly influenced by Nizami, including the best
of them... *Joseph and Zulaikh* and *Layla and Majnun* and *Salman and
Absal* and his mainly prose works *Lawa'ih: A Treatise on Sufism* and
The Beharistan (Abode of Spring). He also composed three *Divans*
consisting of *ghazals, ruba'is, qasidas, qit'as* and other, mainly mystical,
poems... he composed prefaces to each.

Translations from...

*Jami: Selected Poems, Translation & Introduction by Paul; Smith, New
Humanity Books, Campbells Creek, 2008.*

Try hard to keep the secret of your love to yourself:

because he told his, Mansur they were executing.

Jami, pearls from solitude's ocean are to be valued:

the self-absorbed ones aren't worth them receiving.

*

SA'IB (1601-1670). Mirza Muhammad Ali Tabrizi who used the *takhallus* of Sa'ib was born in Isfahan but he loved more the city of Tabriz, the birthplace of his parents where his father was a merchant who moved to Isfahan in the era of Shah Abbas the Great. He went to Mecca, then Kabul… where he was introduced to Shah Jahan. He went to Kashmir, then returned to Isfahan. His fame spread to India and Turkey mainly because he invented new styles of composing poetry, new concepts and philosophical and mystical and Sufi imagery.

Translation from…

The Divine Wine Volume Two, Translations & Introduction by Paul Smith, New Humanity Books, Campbells Creek, 2005.

Love that inflames the world faith and infidelity

is beyond:

my neck the grip of Brahmin's thread and rosary

is beyond.

Mansur's jar of love was empty… so it made much noise,

or, in Unity's winehouse it of all to speak easily,

is beyond.

DARA SHIKOH (1615-1659). He was the oldest son of Emperor Shah Jahan and was known to be a loving husband, a good son and loving father. He was a fine poet, his poems having the influence of Sufism to which he was dedicated. He used 'Qadiri' as his *takhallus* or pen-name. His *Divan* of *ghazals, ruba'is* and *qasidas* in Persian was not the only work he left behind, his five prose works on Sufism and mysticism are popular in India even today. His *Majma al-Bahrain* or *The Mingling of the Two Oceans* is an explanation of the mystical sameness of Sufism and Vedanta. He also translated the *Upanishads, Bhagwad Gita and Yoga-Vasishta* into Persian. He had a great breath of vision and was respected by many of the Sufi Masters of the time such as Shaikh Muhibbullah Allabadi, Miyan Mir and Mulla Badakhshi and the 'naked' Sufi poet Sarmad (to follow). He was greatly loved by his niece Zeb-un-Nissa, the poetess 'Makhfi'. His cruel, fundamentalist brother Emperor Aurangzeb brutally killed him on the 21st of August 1659.

Translation from…

Ruba'iyat of Dara Shikoh, Translation & introduction by Paul Smith, New Humanity Books, Campbells Creek, 2009.

Adam… mankind's father, Satan disowned,

didn't he?

Hallaj said, "I am the Truth" and got killed,

didn't he?

Really, it's the evil and malicious spirit of this priest…

every saint and every prophet he tormented,

didn't he?

MAKHFI (1639-1702). Princess Zeb-un-Nissa... (pen-name 'Makhfi') was the oldest daughter of the Mogul Emperor Aurungzeb of India. She revealed great intelligence from an early age and so received teaching. She discovered she had a remarkable memory and by the age of seven she had like Hafiz become a *hafiz,* one who had learnt the whole of the *Koran* by heart. Her proud father gave an enormous feast to celebrate, all his army in Delhi were feasted and the poor were given gold, businesses were closed for days.

A woman called Miyabai was hired as her teacher and in four years she had learnt Arabic, then mathematics and astronomy. She started to write a commentary on the *Koran* but her father objected and she had to stop. She had written poems from a young age in Arabic but a scholar from Arabia commented, "These are wise and clever poems and it is a miracle that a foreigner knows Arabic so well, but... it is still obvious that they were composed by an Indian." Being a perfectionist, from then on she only composed her poems in Persian.

At first she wrote her poetry in secret but her tutor, a scholar named Shah Rustom Ghazi, found her poems and prophesized her future greatness and went to her father and persuaded him to search India and Persia to find poets and bring them to come to Delhi to become a circle of poets surrounding her. She never married and was eventually imprisoned by her father for many years for being involved in a plot with her brother to unseat him and for her Sufi beliefs. She eventually died in prison.

Translation from...

Makhfi: The Princess Sufi Poet Zeb-un-Nissa, A selection of Poems from her Divan, Translation & Introduction by Paul Smith, New Humanity Books, Campbells Creek, 2006.

My body and soul thirst for Your Love and like Mansur every

grain of this body cries, "We are a part, You're all, we're

Divinity!"

Waves of Your Love's deluge roll over the boat of destruction...

soul drowned in love's depth a Noah could not lift to float

free.

*

BEDIL (1644-1721). Mirza Abdul-Qader Bedil is one of the most respected poets in Afghanistan. In the early 17th century, his family moved from Afghan Turkestan (Balkh region) to India, to live under the Moghul dynasty. Bedil himself, although ethnically an Uzbek, was born and educated in India, near Patna. In his later life he spent time travelling and visiting his ancestral lands. His writings in Persian are extensive. He was greatly influenced by Hafiz. His *Kulliyat* (complete works) consist of many *ghazals, rubai's, tarkib-bands,* a *tarjih-band, mu'ammas* (riddles) and more. He also wrote four *masnavis,* the most important being *Irfaan,* which he completed at age 68. It contains many stories and fairy tales, outlining his philosophical views. Bedil's 16 books of poetry contain nearly 147,000 couplets. With Ghalib he is considered a master of the complicated 'Indian Style' of *ghazal.*

Bedil enjoyed virtually no fame in Iran and only few scholars knew of him until recently. In Afghanistan and Tajikistan however, he had a following that almost followed like a cult. People would get together at weekly Bedil meetings to study and interpret his poetry, and he was the poet of choice for many *ghazal* singers.

Translation from…

Unity in Diversity: Anthology of Sufi and Dervish Poets of the Indian-Subcontinent, Translation & Introduction by Paul Smith, New Humanity Books, Campbells Creek, 2003.

> This feast of madness… so tender and beautiful,
>
> it is;
>
> uproar that creates a Resurrection, loud and full,
>
> it is.
>
> Into thinking of what Mansur said do not go too far:
>
> every mosquito has its own echo… and powerful
>
> it is!

*

RAHMAN BABA (1652-1711). Abdul Rahman (respectfully referred to as Rahman Baba) is considered by many to be the greatest Sufi Pashtun poet to compose poems, mainly *ghazals,* in the Pushtu language.

Rahman Baba was born in the early seventeenth century in the hilly Mohmand region of Afghanistan, outside of Peshwar. He was called 'The Nightingale of Peshwar'. This was a time when Afghanistan was under invasion by the Persians to the west and the Mongols to the east, a period of great struggle and hardship.

Yet, in the midst of this turmoil, the young Abdul Rahman showed himself to be an excellent student with a natural gift for poetry. But as he grew older he became disillusioned, questioning the real value of such pursuits. He withdrew from the world, becoming a hermit, dedicating himself to prayer and devotion. In his solitary worship... he wrote poetry, again.

Despite his reclusive life, Rahman Baba's poetry quickly spread and gained fame. Religious figures used his poetry to inspire the devout. Political leaders used his poems to inspire the independence movement. Rahman Baba's poetry became an important part of the nation's voice.

His *Divan* consists of 343 poems... *ghazals* and a few *qasidas*. Hafiz (many of Rahman's *ghazals* resemble his) and Sana'i were two major influences on him, but also the poems of Rumi, 'Iraqi and Jami.

Translation from...

Rahman Baba: Selected Poems, Translation & Introduction by Paul Smith, New Humanity Books Campbells Creek, 2009.

> This, is the rose and that... is the thorn:
> this is Mansur and the gallows-tree...
> that is.
> This is the beloved, that... malicious one:
> this is the treasure, the viper, deadly...
> that is.

KHWAJA MOHAMMAD (born mid-late 17th C.). The information on this poet is meagre. Little is known about him except that he lived in the reign of the fundamentalist Mughal emperor Aurangzeb and belonged to the Bangash tribe of Afghans who ruled the valley of that name and of which Kohatt is the chief town. Khwaja Mohammad lived the life of a dervish and followed the tenets of the Chishti sect. He was a disciple of Rahman Baba (above), who was a disciple of Mi'an Panju a celebrated Sufi Master who came originally from India and dwelt for many years in Afghanistan.

Khwaja Mohammad Bangash was a man of learning and passed most of his time with his teacher or spiritual guide. He is known to have performed the pilgrimage to Mecca and Medina and after his return he gave up writing poetry. His *Divan* is a very rare book. His *ghazals* in Pushtu are deeply mystical but occasionally he devotes a poem to the remembrance of lost friend.

Translation from...

Tongues on Fire: anthology of Sufi, Dervish, Warrior & court Poets of Afghanistan, Translation & Introduction by Paul Smith, New Humanity Books, Campbells Creek, 2006.

And love has brought scandal both in this world and the next:

on one named Majnun and on the son of Hallaj, named

Mansur.

And what would the hunter in the forest ever know about it,

if the partridge didn't signal him by calling so loud and

clear?

MUSHTAQ (1689-1758). Mir Sayyid Ali Mushtaq of Isfahan was in the literary movement that helped return poetry in the Persian language from the somewhat intricate and complex 'Indian Style'. He was influenced by Iraki, Sadi and Hafiz. It is said that he was the teacher of poetry of the traveller and author of the well-known biography of poets of the time and previous times *Atash-kada* (Fire Temple), Lutf 'Al Beg Adhar. Mushtaq was considered a master of the *ghazal* who brought new life into an old style and trained younger contemporaries besides Lutf and so influenced a whole generation. Many of his poems are mystical.

Translation from…

The Divine Wine, Volume Two, Translation & Introduction by Paul Smith, New Humanity Books, Campbells Creek, 2004.

> You, with a simple heart, who the Truth is speaking;
> you are like Mansur, all others are your foes… lying!
> A treasure is the Truth so when you find it, hide it…
> show it, you'll be responsible for your blood flowing!

Sufis & Dervishes: Their Art and Use of Poetry

It has been said that Adam was the first Sufi and Perfect Master *(Qutub)* and that he was also the first poet as he named everything and so through his 'Adamic Alphabet' (see the *Hebraic Tongue Restored* listed below) all languages were born and so... all poetry. Two of Arabia's most highly regarded scholars of the poetic form also claim he was the father of the poetic form of the *ghazal*.

Sufism is said by many Masters and authors to have always existed since Adam as the esoteric side of each faith that has begun by an appearance of that original Perfect Master coming back as the Rasool, Prophet, Messiah, Avatar, Buddha, etc., whatever that Divine One is called.

Many Perfect Masters *(Qutubs)* were poets and many were not. Many came after the appearance of the Prophet Mohammed and many came before him. But, Sufis and Dervishes were called by those names after he passed from this world. The first 'Sufi' is probably Mohammed's son-in-law Hazrat Ali who composed one of the first *ghazals* ever recorded that essentially sums up the meaning of Sufism and Dervishness...

> You do not know it, but in you is the remedy;
> you cause the sickness, but this you don't see.
> You are but a small form... this, you assume:
> but you're larger than any universe, in reality.
> You are the book that of any fallacies is clear,
> in you are all letters spelling out, the mystery.

You are the Being, you're the very Being... It:

you contain That, which contained cannot be!

I have used both the terms 'Sufis' and 'Dervishes' in this book because some of the poets within called themselves not one but the other and criticized the other, for... during the time that they were alive, having become corrupt and following false masters. Hafiz, for instance, always called himself a Dervish and often when mentioning Sufis in his poetry it was usually to criticise them. During his lifetime in Shiraz there was an extremist Sufi Order led by a false master and Shaikh Ali Kolah who sided with various dictators and subjected the people to a very vicious brand of fundamentalism (see my biog. of Hafiz, *Hafiz of Shiraz* 3 vols. for Hafiz's almost lifelong clash with this false Sufi). By the 13th Century many Sufi Orders had become corrupt and full of various dogmas, useless rituals and power hungry and hypocritical shaikhs and false masters. Those who called themselves 'Dervishes' then really meant 'true Sufis'.

The first Sufi and Dervish poets composed in Arabic even though some of them, including the famous and infamous Sufi martyr Mansur Hallaj, were originally from Persia... he was from near Shiraz. From the 10th to the 15th century the vast majority of Sufi and Dervish and other poets in the region composed in Persian, a few in the new languages of Turkish and Urdu and some like Kabir in Hindi; after that... the languages most used by the most conscious and influential poets were Pashtu, Urdu, Punjabi and Sindhi, as the stream of God-consciousness moved originally from Arabia and Egypt to Iraq and Syria then into Iran and Afghanistan and Turkey and finally into the Indian Sub-Continent.

To follow this golden thread of Spiritual Poetry one must follow the true Spiritual Hierarchy of real Saints and God-realized Souls... Perfect Masters, their lives and stories are to be found in the many books listed below and in many others.

What is the essential belief and philosophy of the Sufi and Dervish Masters and Poets? To put it as simply as possibly... The Love of God, the belief in God in human form, the love and respect for all of God's Creation and to try to not hurt anyone or thing. And of course a belief in Truth, Love and Beauty as the greatest of the Divine Attributes. A belief similar, if not the same as the Christian Mystics and Vedantists and believers in the inner way of most religions.

Further Reading...

The Way of the Mystics: The Early Christian Mystics and The Rise of the Sufis by Margaret Smith, Sheldon Press, 1976.
In the Garden of Myrtles: Studies in Early Islamic Mysticism by Tor Andrae, Translated by Birgitta Sharpe. State University of New York Press, Albany. 1987.
Muslim Saints and Mystics... Episodes from the 'Memorial of the Saints' by Farid al-Din Attar, Translated by A.J. Arberry. Routledge and Kegan Paul, London, 1966.
Kashf Al-Mahjub of Al-Hujwiri. Translated by R.A. Nicholson, Luzac, London. 1967.
The Doctrine of the Sufis by Abu Bakr al-Kalabadhi, Translated by A.J. Arberry, Cambridge University Press 1935.
The Mystics of Islam by Reynold A. Nicholson. Routledge and Kegan Paul, London, reprint 1974.
The Idea of Personality in Sufism by Reynold Alleyne Nicholson, First Published 1923.

The Heritage of Sufism Volume One... Edited by Leonard Lewisohn, Oneworld Publications, Oxford, 1999.

Persian Mysticism by R.P. Masani, Award Publishing House, New Delhi, 1981.

An Introduction to Sufi Doctrine by Titus Burkhardt, Trans. by D.M. Matheson. Sh. Muhammad Ashraf, Lahore, 1973.

Persian Sufi Poetry: An Introduction to the Mystical Use of Classical Poems by J.T.P. De Bruijn. Curzon Press, 1997.

The Drunken Universe: An Anthology of Persian Sufi Poetry, Translation and Commentary by Peter Lamborn Wilson and Nasrollah Pourjavady. Phanes Press, Grand Rapids, 1987.

The Persian Sufis by Cyprian Rice, O.P. George Allen and Unwin Ltd, London, 1964.

God Speaks: The Theme of Creation and Its Purpose by Meher Baba. Dodd, Mead & Company, New York, 1955. [Meher Baba in great detail explains the Involution of the Soul and the seven stages of the Spiritual Path, the role of the Perfect Master, the Creation and the different States of God using quotations from Sufi poets and Masters and Sufi terminology and cross-referencing with Christian Mystical and Vedantic terminology. Meher Baba also quotes various couplets by Hafiz when describing the passage through the inner planes of consciousness to God-Realization].

Hallaj teaching.

73

Qit'as...

Yes, go and tell, for the deep Sea I sailed,

that my ship has gone down, far offshore.

By Holy Cross I must go to death of me,

to the Holy Cities I can go to... no more.

I searched the world for a place to call home,

but upon the earth no such a place did I see.

My desires I obeyed and they trapped me...

if with my fate I was contented, I'd be free!

Hear my sorrow, O You, for souls whose witness now:

leave, to go beyond, until into the Witness of Eternity!

Hear my sorrow, O You... for the miracles whose logic

shut argument's mouth, in name of Your love's ardency!

O hear my sorrow... O You... for all of those who rode

themselves as steeds... all the bravery of silent chivalry:

for all them who have been lost, like that vanished tribe

of Ad and their lost Garden of Iram: gone, completely!*

And, after them, the abandoned herd... wandering and

stumbling, blinder than beasts, or she-camels may be!

*Note: The garden of Iram was said to have been created by King Shudad, the son of Ad who was the grandson of Iram, who was the son of Shem, Noah's son. The tribe of Ad settled in the desert near Aden and Ad started to build a fabulous city that was finished by his son Shudad. Shudad created a wonderful garden around his palace that he thought would rival the Garden of Paradise. When it was finished he set out to admire it and when he came near to it all were destroyed by a great sound that came from God. It is said that the ruins still exist near Aden. This poem is said to have been recited by Hallaj on the night before his execution.

If you met me tonight in clothes of real poverty,

be assured that by being on my back threadbare,

this clothing has bestowed on me, real Freedom;

so do not be misled, if you see me like this, here,

different from the past: I have a soul and it must

either perish or rise to a destiny beyond compare.

Wanting the truth, I thought hard about the religions...
I discovered that one root with many branches are they.
It makes good sense not to make one follow a religion...
in case it stops any one from root that in depth does lay.
So, allow that root to claim that one, that root where all
meanings and perfection are opened... to be clear, as day.

O my only One, make me one with You, for no way

can reach Your Oneness, even faith can't hold sway.

The Truth I am… Truth, and the Truth is the Truth,

clothed in Its Essence, separation can't have its way.

See manifested the dawn's light from Your Presence

shining brilliantly, a lightning flash, from every ray!

You live inside my heart; in there are secrets about You:

Your house is good; no, good is the One found by You!

The only secret in there is You, there's no other I know:

with Your Vision look, other than You is one there too?

Whether the night of separation should be short or long,

my closest friend is my hope of You, remembering You.

I'm so happy if it makes You happy to be destroying me

because whatever You choose, my Killer... I choose too!

Heart of You is where a Name of Yours is hidden,

and it is not perceived by light nor by the darkness,

and on seeing light of Your face I see the Mystery:

all Goodness and all Excellence, all Mercifulness.

Beloved, take now this word of mine: You know it,

but the Tablet doesn't; and Pen, not yet, I confess!

This soul of mine had different desires…
but since seeing You they jelled into one.
Those I envied now envy me, as I'm lord
of others, since You my Lord did become.
Due to You they scolded me, my friends,
foes, ignorantly… trying of me, was done.
I have left to men their religion and world
for Your Love, my world and my religion!

I feel no separation… distance from You I do not feel:

it's now my belief that near or far are the same thing.

For me, if I'm separated from You, it's my companion:

not only that, but… as we are one, can it be existing?

Praise to You for where You are from in Your essence;

to Your pure servant, who only to You is prostrating.

You've gone from me but not yet from my conscience,

inside it You're all of my joy and all of my happiness.

When You went, leaving was Your going to leave me

because for me absence became the same as presence,

because You stay in the secret thoughts inside of me,

there... beyond imagination, hidden in my conscience.

It's true that You are my closest friend in the daytime

and I intimately talk with You, through the darkness.

Your will be done, my Lord and my Master!

Your will be done, my purpose and meaning!

O essence of my being, O goal of my desire:

O my speech, O my hints and my gesturing!

O All of my all, O my hearing and my sight,

O my whole, my element, my atoms uniting!

Your place inside my heart is all of my heart:

there is no room for any others in Your place.

Between skin and bone my soul You placed,

what could I do, if I lost You... You replace?

I wrote, but did not write to You… writing
to my Soul what cannot be written I wrote.
Between You as Soul and one who loves it
there's no difference, it's You by me. Note,
that naught I wrote… it all comes from You
to You, replying to You: no answer I quote.

Your Love, I hold with all of my being... You
are my sanctuary: to me You're showing You,
like You are inside me, and if I am turning my
heart to another, that I see some alien is true:
so, I realize my ease with You: me as in life's
prison, men surrounding, so take me... to You!

The Lights in humans are from Lights of religion's Light,

and the Secret is the Secrets in the souls secret insight...

and in all beings is the Being, the Being that says, "BE!"

This heart of mine is chosen, reserved... with it, so tight!

Think deeply upon what I say with the eye of the mind...

the mind is so wanting to be hearing and to have insight!

I've found You within me, yet my tongue calls You:

united in one way, we are also separated in another.

For, while Your majesty conceals You from my eyes,

deep inside my heart ecstasy has brought You closer.

O You, subtle Secret of my secret… You are veiled
from all beings imagination on which life's prevailed:
still, inside and out You have completely manifested
Yourself in each thing to each thing that has existed.
It would be ignorance for me to ask anything of You,
it'd be to doubt, obviously, lack of You being trusted!
O You Absolute Existence, You are not other than I:
how can I possibly for myself, from me… have asked?

With the eye of my heart I saw my Creator:

I said, "Who are You?" You replied, "You!"

So… like from You, there is nowhere… and

there is no where too, when it is about You!

No image You reveal, for one to imagine…

imagination needs to imagine where is You!

That One is You, Who filled Everywhere…

and beyond where, too… so, where are You?

My annihilation's end is in my annihilation,

and in my annihilation is discovered… You!

Whoever seeks God, taking his intellect for a guide,

remaining perplexed God sends him away… so far:

with wild confusion He confounds his inmost heart,

so that distraught he cries, "I know not, *if* You are!"

Your Soul, is mixed with my soul...

like musk is mixed with ambergris,

when perfumes blend: so, what You

touch touches me... we are, together!

O you who go on blaming me for loving that One,

how hard you can be, still are: O if only you knew

how that One helps, you would me never blame...

others have their pilgrimage... and I have one too,

to that Guest in me: they may be offering animals

as a sacrifice... that I offer blood of heart, is true!

There are a people who not by the feet go around:

they circle God, are all excused from *Kaaba*, too!

Is there anything on earth that is without You
that they would go up to Heaven to You see?
Dazzled by Your light You see them looking,
their sight is so lost that You they do not see!

If the shadow has got you in its grip...

then out into light of heart's peace go.

If who you are you don't know... lost,

listen to Beloved, "I am you, know!"

Your name you'll forget, and home...

know you are no one, found: it is so!

Found, but not by one who will brag

of such many rescues... O no, O no!

Found by One who reveals nothing

and secretly guides, to Love's flow!

At heart one may throw a blood-red

rose; symbol of separation long ago!

O my God, with this illness what am I to do?

When doctors see me coming, they're leaving!

They shout out, "Let your sickness, cure you!"

With sickness, can one who is sick, be curing?

O God, because of Love I've become so tired:

about this, how can I, to You be complaining?

This pain that I have is from soul's suffering:

it's I, myself... this sickness goes on causing!

Glory to that One Who humanity created

as the secret of His Divine Light, shining.

And then that One was appearing for His

creation in form of one eating and drinking.

Until that One's creatures glanced at Him

that from one eyebrow to another, is going!

Love, in pre-eternity, from the very start...

from inside it and due to it, it is appearing.

Love, before time began, is an attribute of

that One, Whose victims now are living!

They, are from in that One, beyond time:

while the transitory on time is depending.

That One summoned Love upon creation

as an attribute, so... a spark was shining.

With *Alif* as partner, *Lam* was formed...

both, as One, were before the beginning!

In separating them they are two to unite,

as with slave and Lord they are differing.

Truly, desire's fire with Truth enflames...

no matter how near or far, they are being.

The more infatuated, the more they fade;

the strong are humbled, if hearts losing.

Note: This poem refers to the Covenant that God made on the First Day i.e. before the Creation, in God's Imagination. God created (in His Infinite Imagination) all the souls that were possible to create, and He asked them: "Am I NOT your God?" This of course was something of a trick question, and not without a sense of humour. Some, out of love, not wishing to be rude by not answering answered: "Yes!" (In other words: You are NOT our God). These were the lovers of God. Others did not answer. God then manifested all of the souls into creation, some of them being lovers, and others, those who had to learn from the lovers to try to love and to say "yes" to God, even though to try is the best that one can do.

Love that's hidden is continually at risk...

from confronting fears, comes true peace.

If one talks about love that is kept secret,

it's like the fire in stone hiding... useless!

And when the police and the jailor arrive,

tellers of tales about me go on telling lies.

I feel like I want to be freed of Your love,

but I'd need to not hear or to see, no less!

Friend, you played; time's gone to play with old heads:

you won game, broke heart's secret, but time's healing.

These eyes wherein desires used to grow, are dimmed;

heart, where love's memories fought, are not fighting.

You're there now, pulled down with the enemies, lost:

you do not visit here anymore, so you I am not seeing.

The same way the donkey went carrying Umm 'Amr:

she never came back again, donkey wasn't returning.

In eye of my heart I did see my Lord...
I said, "Without a doubt it's truly You.
In everything it is only You that I see,
through all I see nothing but You, too.
Every place that exists You only own;
and yet... that no place is You, is true!
Still, if You were to designate a place,
there, would give information on You!
If You, there was a way of imagining;
imagination, it would know You, too.
I understand all, so all that I'm seeing
as 'I' am annihilated, can be only You!
O Lord, please bless and forgive me...
for that I'm seeking only You is true!"

My heart's disturbed due to four letters,

also my longing and mind and grieving:

Alif... by which actions are stimulated,

Lam: that one towards guilt is leading.

Lam... my meaning is increased by it...

Ha... makes me understand, be loving. *

*Note: These four letters are spelling out 'Allah'.

Calm followed by silence, then words by accident:
then comes knowledge, drunkenness, obliteration!
Earth is followed by fire, and then light appears…
from cold shade's appearing, then sun shines upon.
A road of thorns, a path appears and wilderness…
now a river appears, then ocean, a shore to step on.
And then there is contentment, longing, then love,
and then there's nearness, loving, then unification.
Then closing followed by opening… then nothing:
then being apart, together, then… desire comes on!
These are the signs for those who can understand,
who the world as almost worthless they look upon.

O You sun, O You moon, You daytime...

my heaven and my hell is You, only You!

It would be sinful to give up for You, sin!

Anyone leaving You would be empty, too!

They for You give away all begging ways,

but what of the one who can't help it, too?

I'm astonished at me and You;

O You, goal of all my longing!

You let me, to You come close,

though You 'me' I was calling.

Finding You, I was losing me:

in You, me You were effacing!

You are the blessing of my life

and after death my consoling!

Only You, are caring for me...

my fear You go on comforting.

You, are the garden of Truth...

now, my talents are blooming!

If there's anything that I want

that desire is... You be having!

There's a pearl in the depth of my heart,

it's a pearl that can't be touched by me.

And, when doubts steal into my mind,

I begin to tremble... something terribly.

My Beloved, has given to me this as a

present to keep in confidence, secretly.

And by it I'm able to see, though blind:

I'm given wisdom though I act naively.

This love by 'seven sleepers' is known:

those seven are friends, I hold dearly. *

In the shadow of their mountain time

is stopping like it has stopped for me!

My Beloved, returns in its silence…

comes back to claim pearl, rightfully!

*Note: Seven Sleepers, refers to Christian youths who hid inside a cave in a mountain outside the city of Ephesus around 250 AD, to escape a persecution of the Roman emperor Decius. Having fallen asleep in the cave, they awoke approximately 150-200 years later. The story has its highest prominence in the Muslim world; it is told in the Koran (18, 9-26) While not giving the number of youths involved, the story largely parallels the Christian account. This version includes a dog that accompanied the youths into the cave, and kept watch at the entrance for the entire time.

Lamp of the Divine Light is the science of Prophecy...

ecstatic inspiration's spark is in grave God digs for it!

By God, breathing into my skin's breath of His Spirit,

breathing a note that Israfil will blow, to end this pit!*

When One is transformed before my soul so as to talk

to me, upon Mt Sinai I see Moses... in my ecstatic fit!

*Note: Israfil, the Angel of the Trumpet, holds his holy trumpet to his lips century after century, awaiting the signal from God to sound it at the Last Judgment.

Between me and the Truth, there is no longer
explanation, or proof, or signs to convince me.
A vision of God is shining here... like a flame
that's magnificent in its shining sovereignty!
One only knows God to who God is known:
an illusion that passes, can't know Divinity.
In other words, the Creator cannot be taken
from what the Creator creates... obviously!
Can't you see, a passing being turned away
from that One is away... for all of Eternity?
The One is proof, from the One, to the One
and in the One is the Witness, essentially...
of the Reality in the Revelation that can tell,
can perceive what's good, what's evil totally.
God is the proof, from God, in God, for God:
in Truth we found It, in Its outer form we see.
This is my existence, my evidence, my belief:
this is the Oneness, explaining God's Unity!
In this way we express our being One in God,
we who all know the One openly and secretly.
This is the height of all intoxicated by God...
the people of God, soul's companions... of me!

Now, becoming evident to you...

is a well-kept secret's revelation.

On your darkness a dawn breaks:

your heart's veil, the secret upon!

God wouldn't be revealed to you

if you kept to yourself, on and on.

But when you destroy your heart

God enters, gives His revelation.

With this, a dialogue will follow,

its words to Us taste to chew on.

In creation, there are hearths and fires of faith,

and in hearts that can keep secrets, conscience.

For Being in depth of us beings is the creating

Existence, holding heart that wants Essence!

What I am saying with mind's eye consider...

as the mind can listen, see, know consequence!

O friend I've been immersed in a deep sea,

I'm not Husayn, as him don't think of me!

See me as near God, I am God, I am God!

From all greed, hatred and pride I am free!

'I don't blame me as blame from me is far:
please help me Lord because alone is me!
True, is the promise; Your promise is true
and hard at the beginning of my destiny!'
Here is my letter needing to be inscribed:
read it and then know that I a martyr be!

I try to hard to be waiting patiently...
but this heart, can it ever be patient?
To mine Your spirit has joined itself
in closeness, and in being... distant.
And so it's true that I'm You as You
are me and that which I always want.

I wish for You, but not to get a reward...

to get punishment for You I am wishing.

From all of this I obtained what I desire,

except for joy of my passion in suffering.

One night the sun rose up of the One I love,

it shone on and about setting nothing knew:

because the sun of the day enhances night...

and the sunbird of the heart away new flew.

Passions of the Truth that are entirely born of Truth,

but… that cannot attain the highest understanding:

what is passion but an inclination followed by a look,

that among those minds the flame goes on spreading?

And if Truth should come and then inhabit the mind

three states increase compared to those of foreseeing:

a state that annihilates mind in essence of its desire,

then renders one into a state that's deeply confusing;

a state where all forces of the mind becomes knotted

on turning to a sight annihilating all who are seeing.

Ah, you breeze, to the gazelle be saying...

"My thirst will be worse from drinking!"

I've a Beloved, His love, guts surround...

and if He wants, on them He's treading.

His spirit is my spirit, my soul His soul:

He wishes I wish, I wish He is wishing!

I never stop floating in the sea of love,

up and down the waves are lifting me.

Sometimes those waves lift me up and

sometimes I'm choosing to be gloomy.

Then finally He is leading me to love,

there... where there is no shore to see.

I call Him Whose Name I do not tell,

and Who in love isn't betrayed by me.

What my love doesn't wish for, Lord,

is not in our pact... and will never be.

When I remember You, nostalgia almost kills me
and my absence from You is grief… and sadness.
Each part of me is now a heart that implores You,
that quickly succumbs to pain, grief and distress.

Ghazals...

By God I'm swearing the sun never sets or is rising

when out of love for You, each breath I'm breathing.

And, when ever I go off with friends to have a talk,

as we sit, about You is the one thing I'm discussing.

And all my thoughts are only on You, happy or sad:

only You are in my heart; "You," I'm remembering.

And when I'm thirsting I don't think to drink water

unless… in that cup that face of Yours I am seeing!

And, if I could possibly come to You, then I would

rush, either on my face, or even on my head walking.

Is it I, or is it You? The two, gods numbering two!

It is not up to me to be claiming that there are two!

For eternity is Your Self, in the nothingness of me:

the Everything that is mine, knows illusion as two!

Your Essence is where? From where am I to identify

when nowhere is mine… that, is really obvious, too?

And Your face, which with my eyesight I may seek,

either in the vision of my heart… or eyes sight too?

Between You and me is an 'I AM' overcoming me…

using Your 'I AM' take mine, from between us, too.

I've a Beloved I visit when I am alone completely,

He is always available though Him one can't see.

You will never see me lending an ear to that One

to be listening to any words He might say openly,

because His words have no form, are not spoken...

and, they are not like any voices making a melody.

It is like I am my own go-between, communicating

through my inspiration with my essence, inwardly!

That One is here, away, near and distant: to try to

describe or encompass Him, is... an impossibility!

Imagine, that One is nearer than one's conscience,

and even than inspiration's flashes... closer, in me!

See... I'm here, O You, my secret, my surety:

see, I'm here, O You my goal, the end of me!

I call to You... no, You're calling me to You:

can I talk to You, if You'd not talked to me?

You are my soul's Essence, what I aim for...

You cause me to speak, O my voice, all I see!

You're the All of my all, my ear and eyesight:

You are my everything, my parts, my totality!

O Everything of my everything, my enigma...

I try to tell All, the profound I say unclearly!

From You, soul was before, dying of ecstasy:

that promise You made me will be end of me!

O Guest, O You One Whom I wait upon...

O soul's food, Life in both worlds, obviously.

My eyes, my ears, may heart be my ransom!

Why do I have to wait to be alone... tell me?

Although You are before eyes You're hidden:

my heart sees You from my lack of proximity.

O You, You are the One that I am seeking,

and in my heart that One that I'm desiring.

Absolute Being, You're the Complete One,

Who I with each bit or part of me, is loving!

From grief and longing I am turning to You:

for You my heart is in claws of a bird, flying.

Lost in shock, rocked by the agony I am in…

from one wilderness to another, I am going.

By Your mystery I'm blinded as I travel on,

it is always moving… as fast as lightning!

It could be likened to a vision's quickness…

that after one's waking up, is disappearing.

By that river of consciousness, taken off…

for, that Absolute Being needs satisfying.

With the eye of knowledge I direct my sight,

I've not a single doubt that my sight is right.

Far away from any meaning or doubting too,

this one's conscience is purified by the light!

On the waves of thinking I'm moving along,

I am like an arrow that has a target in sight.

With the wings of longing my heart's flying,

by the wind of my aim I'm traveling... light!

To the One I go Whom I'm afraid to talk of;

not saying Who, in riddles, I hide my plight.

I roam the desert until beyond all limits I go,

but... not over the edge, I know what's right!

Then to that One's Will I bow like a slave...

with Love heart is branded: *ah,* such might!

In such closeness my true self I then lose...

so who I am, I am made to forget, outright!

When, over you is riding the steed of loneliness...
and swallowing all hope is despair's cry, no less;
into your left hand take the armour of humility...
into your right hand be taking the spear of tears!
It's important, to be of your lower self cautious...
watchful of its unseen retribution causing stress.
When, in the darkness you must be going along,
under the lamp of purity, be sheltering... no less!
Say to Beloved, "See, my shattered condition...
before we are destined to meet forgive my mess!
O my Beloved, from me don't be far, separated;
before the end don't give up on me, me... bless!"

Ruba'is...

I'm the One I love, the One I love is

me,

we are two spirits that live... in one

body.

If you see me, then... you see that One...

and, if you see that One... both, you

see.

A secret, hidden for a long time, is told to

you…

from the dark of night, from you, a day dawns

too:

the veil of the heart over its secret mystery is

you,

it would never have been sealed if not for you,

too.

In denying You, it is You I sanctify;

my reason in You, is madness, say I.

Who's Adam, if that one isn't You?

Who in the banished Satan does lie?

A sense of You call the souls to You,

and a proof of You is all proof of You!

My heart has eyes that at You look...

that all is now in Your hands, is true!

My host was generous as I was entertained

at the high table... but as cups were passed,

he called for winding-sheet and the scimitar:

to drink with dragon in summer is so fated.*

*Note: This was the final poem Hallaj uttered.

Qasidas...

My faithful friends... kill me,
to kill me is to alive make me.
To destroy all trace of my life
is my highest goal... you see.
To stay in my lower self, is a
a sin I cannot of repenting be.
My life, due to my lower self,
is destroyed: I'm lost, totally!
So, my friends, take my life...
burn my poor bones, entirely!
Then, when by my corpse they
walk in graveyards unhappily,
they will find Friend's secret,
in the inner folds... it will be!
I am a shaikh at one moment
and one of the highest degree,
then I'm a small child who on
a nurse is depending entirely.
Or, I am in a box fast asleep,
under the black earth lies me.
My mother birthed her father
it was a wonder that I did see.

And my daughters that I made
like this were the sisters of me,
not in this world full of time…
nor, by any thing like adultery!
So, get together all the parts…
bits of forms that shine to see,
or, that of air, and of fire too…
some water without impurity,
and sow all in soil that's dry…
then watering it from cups be,
of maids that lovingly serve…
streams, flowing refreshingly.
And when seven days pass by
a perfect plant will grow to see!

I am here O my secret, true One, You can see me!

You called me and I came, O my hope and reality!

I go on calling to You... no, it is You to me calling:

Am I saying it is You, or, You saying, "It's Me"?

You're as far as I have to go, Spring of all springs:

You're my reason for being, all my words set free!

All that I am You are, all I see and I hear is You...

You are the universe and the smallest thing to me.

You are totality of what I am and a mystery it is:

the small thing I am confuses You, so hard to see!

You I've always loved and at times I've been hurt

when You've let You to be love's prisoner, in me.

Though I choose to be, I mourn for being an exile:

because of the grief I have my enemies are happy.

I am excited by being afraid as I get close to You:

in depth of my heart it is my longing calming me.

With this One I love so much, what am I to do?

All the doctors tell me from my illness they flee!

I'm weakened, consumed by this love for God...

how to say to that One, "You, did this to me"?

My heart sees when I look but how to be telling
the ways of that One, but by actions... silently?
It's this 'I' of mine that's wrong, a woeful thing!
I am the creator of this condition... this, agony!
I am like someone who is drowning in the ocean
who is reaching out for help with fingertips only.
That one alone who has reached depth of heart,
only that one reaches depth of such melancholy.
You know what I know in this unending illness:
in Yours... I'll find death and resurrection of me.
O You, my hope, my prayers, my abode, breath:
You... my religion and in the end my Destiny...
tell me, "I've saved you!" O my eyes and ears...
why, do You still keep me away, in this agony?
Even though, to my sight You remain hidden...
still my heart can off in the distance, You... see!

The Tawasin

From the Light of the Invisible

a lamp was shining.

It came and it shone

and returned to the Invisible.

It was the Light of all lights

beyond all lights,

and it was the Moon

of all moons.

Its Light was beyond the heavens

surrounded by mystery.

God named that one*

'unlettered'

due to that one's intensity,

and because that one was of

the *Kaaba*

and the state of that one

was never

changing.

*Note: The Prophet Mohammed.

That one's breast was unlimited,

power expanded...

will was authorized!

And so,

the burden oppressing

that one

was lifted away.

And so,

that moon was revealed to all

and that full moon

out from clouds of Yamama

shone...

and in the land of Mecca

the sun of the morning

shone

and that lamp shone

from the light of

Divine Wisdom

and Grace.

Whatever

that one

said

from wisdom

was said

in light,

in spirit,

in these six things…

that one

was present…

in insight,

in the eye that sees,

in a warning,

showing

the way,

that one

made a limit

on conduct.

No one

has seen that one

in Reality

except for

Siddaq the Sincere*

who

knew that one

to be

the real one…

who

remained true to

that one,

who walked

with that one,

and no other

could separate

those two.

*Note: Abu Bakr.

No seeker found

that one,

nor knew

that one

and

that one's purity

has stayed unknown

as it was so pure

it was not created.

"We have given

that one the Book

and they have known

that one

as they knew

their sons,

and that one

reveals

the Truth."*

(Koran 2: 141)

And

from light of

that one

there came

the light

of all prophecy

and

from rays of light of

that one

new rays of light

were coming.

And,

no other light

is brighter,

more clear,

older...

than the light

of

that one.

The meditation of

that one

surpassed all others,

that one's being

was beyond all being,

that one's name

was better than the Pen

for that one

was first in this world,

beyond this world.

That one

is the most charming,

generous and kind,

most wise, deepest…

that one is Mohammed,

all praise is that one's,

that one's word is most praised,

endures most,

unique in mind,

purity, generosity.

The One

made that one

beyond all others,

above all else,

raising that one above all…

that one

was proclaimed the greatest,

known over the earth and sea..

so bright, so full of light,

most powerful…

one who sees all,

who understands.

Before creation existed

that one existed,

was known.

And,

from beginning to end

the name of

that one

is written upon time.

The essence of

that one

is purifying,

the word of

that one

is warning,

the knowledge of

that one

is inspiring.

Speech of

that one is Arabic,

but tribe of that one

is not in east or west...

whom that one comes from

and who comes from

that one

should be esteemed,

for in the Sacred House

is this Friend.

The sign made by

that one

opened eyes to all secrets

and all became known to

even the ordinary.

The One

made that one speak...

it was the Truth

and that one was free.

That one is the Truth in form.

The heart of that one

was cleaned of all darkness.

That one came with a Word

not created or invented,

untouched by the tongue.

That one came with the Word

that never changes,

is the Truth,

outside the mind...

the End of all ends.

Above

that one

the cloud was lifting

then it was revealing...

under the feet of

that one

lighting was flashing,

dark was disappearing.

And the cloud

let go the rain,

the earth was fruitful.

Compared to ocean of

that one

all knowledge

is a drop of water,

all wisdom

is a swallow of water

from the deep river of

that one.

All beyond time

written down,

is a moment

in the time of

that one.

The One

is with

that one

in Reality.

What can be measured

and what can not

is with

that one.

In Reality

that one

is the first...

the last

in the line

of

Messengers.

That one

is creation's secret,

knowledge of the Essence

in form.

But,

no one

who

is seeking

knowledge

has reached

that one,

and

no one

who is

judging

has ever

beheld

the wisdom

of

that one.

The One

never

brought

that one

to

that

which is created,

for

the One

is

that one,

yet

where

is the One?

And so,

wherever

that one

is,

is

the One.

And,

knowing

or knows is knowing,

has been beyond

the 'm' in Mohammed...

one is caught in there.

And,

anyone

who can move

has been further than

the 'h' in Mohammed...

'h' will lead to the second 'm'

and the letter 'd'

will bring one

back

to the first 'm'

of

Mohammed.

The One

made Word of

that one

be manifested…

and the warning of

that one

all heard

and all were speechless.

The *Koran* came out

and tongue of

that one

was fluent,

illuminating,

empowering hearts.

All who stood with

that one

stood true,

proclaiming

the greatness of

that one.

And,

if you were to leave,

escape

to a land far off…

far away

from

that one,

no way

will you discover

what is true,

and none will guide you.

For you

sick soul,

will find none

to save you!

Talk of the most wise

in this world

is like sand

before

that one.

Reality

cannot be known by

the created being in illusion,

and Reality

is not linked to mind,

to thoughts of things

made in the illusion.

Those thoughts,

that come and disappear

are never able

to be reaching

Reality.

Its knowledge

is so profound,

how can they reach it?

The One,

is beyond Reality

and the 'Truth'

can't describe

the One.

The moth

flies around candle's light

all through the night

until morning comes

with the sun...

and

that moth

goes off to tell

to the others,

what happened,

or the state

of that moth...

and in what occurred

was happiness,

much joy,

for in the heart of

that moth

is the desire

to gain

perfect union.

The light

of

the flame

is

knowledge

of

Reality.

The heat

of the flame

is

the

reality

of the

Reality:

knowing

it.

To enter its heat

and know its light

is...

the Truth.

The moth isn't satisfied

with the candle's light,

with the candle's heat...

so,

into the flame

it flies.

Its companions wait,

and good news brought

back

is what was seen

and how to live through it.

What was seen

was preferred to

what was heard.

That one

became non-being,

consumed

into worthless

tiny particles,

fragments.

So,

in this present form

that one

now survives,

with no name,

with no form,

with no sign,

no symbol.

You ask

how is this possible?

How did

that one

come back to friends?

That one

reaching the state of sight

needs no more to hear news

of love...

that one

is even far beyond

the state of seeing.

These things

are beyond

those who act

through instinct

or desire,

who

cannot

think straight

who are wearing sin

as clothes

for

mortal life...

such

as these

will not discover

as

this one has.

O

if you think

in such a state

as this one has,

or will soon be reaching,

or in the past

have already reached,

O

no, no, no!

this one is on the way

to discover

the One,

the way leading to

the One.

O,

this one belong to

the One

but the One

this one is not yet.

O,

if you want to know,

then know this...

only Mohammed

knows

Reality,

and Mohammed

is not the father

of any man

but is God's

last

Messenger.

That one

went beyond

jinn and men,

to where

there

was no longer

error!

There,

that one

came closer,

to a distance of

two-bows length

or closer…

and when

that one

reached

the knowledge

of Reality

that one

received news of it

in the heart.

When

that one

came to the Truth,

before

the Merciful One

that one

bowed down saying;

"My mind
bows before You
and my heart
belongs to You."
When the End of all ends
was reached
that one said…
"No words exist
to praise You properly,
no language
can describe You."
At Reality of the real
that one said…
"You are the
only One
capable
of praising You
as You
should be!"

Then

that one,

let go all desire

for the physical,

illusory world

and

the Throne

that one

did come to,

and the heart of

that one

saw truly...

and close to

the Tree

that was the

boundary of Knowledge,

beyond which none goes...

the eyes of

that one

never failed!

Reality

is subtle,

sharp and edged...

the path

to it

is

n

a

r

r

o

w

with

flames,

fires burning

low and high

of all types,

and

beyond

is a field

of wilderness,

dark,

uninhabited...

and

the stranger

follows

that path

and

experiences

forty states,

stations,

and

then

the stranger

tells

about

what happened

there.

For every state

there are

manners

of thinking,

ways

of discovering,

some

easy to be

learning,

some

easy to be

knowing

and

some

beyond,

so far

beyond

understanding.

And,

then

the stranger

goes into

the wilderness

and

stays there,

then

goes beyond

that desert...

and

knows no one

and

no one owns,

and

mountains and rocks,

hills and plains

are not

obstacles.

When Moses

the time had done,

his family he left

and Reality

was all he knew…

with what he knew

he was satisfied,

for he preferred

hearing

rather than

seeing…

this made him

different

to 'the Best of Men'

(Mohammed),

so,

he said:

"Perhaps

I'll come with

news!"

And,

when

that Guide

with indirect

information

was satisfied

with

it,

then

those

who followed

were satisfied

with seeking

it

from

signs

and

symbols.

Upon

Mount Sinai…

the

burning bush!

And,

what Moses

heard

was from

that bush…

or,

not that bush,

but

the

One!

And so,

this one

is

like

that

burning bush!

And,

what

this one says

is not mine

but

from

the One!

And so,

Reality

is what

is Real,

and

what is created

is something

made up.

And so,

give up

created things

to be

the One,

and so

the One

can be

you

in

Reality.

And so,

this one is seeing

the attribute

and the attribute

tells of

the attribute…

and so,

is contained

within

the Reality…

and so,

who is

that

one?

The One

said

to Moses:

"You

are guiding

to the

Proof,

not

to its object,

the One

already

proven.

I am

the Proof

of

all

proof."

The One

allowed

this one

to see

the Reality

by

a promise

affirmed

by

word of mouth,

and

this one told it

though in

this heart

this one knew

this one shouldn't...

but,

the secret is

beyond

Reality.

The One

gave this one

the secret,

knowledge,

in

this one's heart

and

gave to this one

that knowledge

in this one's

own tongue,

and…

the One,

drew this one close

and

this one's separation

finished

and

this one became

the intimate one.

The first circle

or door

in the world of illusion

is one

that leads

to

the One,

and

the second circle

is the person

who

reaches the circle,

and

the third circle

is

what has

reached

Reality

and

in the wilderness

was lost.

Through

the first circle

one can reach

the One…

through

the second circle

all

will be lost…

through

the third

woods, deserts,

wilderness.

In the first circle

is

no opening,

but…

in the heart

of

that circle,

see

the point,

that

is longing

for

Reality

that

does not

destroy things,

physical or invisible,

seen by eyes

or

by soul known,

unchanging,

creating.

And,

if you wish

to understand

what this one has

explained,

then

"take four birds

and tame them

to

turn to you,"*

for

the One

never

flies!

Note: Koran 2:260

It is

the jealousy

of

the One

that

makes the One

be here

when absent.

It is

the awe,

the power

of

the One

that

obstructs,

bewilderment

that

stops us.

These,

are the meanings

of Reality…

more subtle

and more sharp

are the meanings

when

the judgment

is suspended

and

one

is

longing,

bitterly,

for

the

meaning.

This

is

because

one

is

looking

on

all

sides

of

the

circle

and

not

beyond

it...

from

inside

it.

And,

the

knowledge

of

the One,

the

Truth,

is

pure

is

sacred,

and

the

circle

is

the

circle

of

the

Divinity.

Because of this

that one

was named

the Pure

and

the Sacred,

and

from

the circle

of

the

Sacred

that one

came

out.

The One

is still

beyond

whatever

is...

but,

that one

wearing

the garment

of Truth

went out

and sighed

"Ahhhh,"

to

all of

creation.

Now,

much deeper

and

more difficult

is this explanation

of

the

Point

.

It

is the

Source

that

never grows,

never decreases,

never ceases

to

be.

Any one

who

disbelieves,

says no

to

the Point,

is

in the first

circle...

not believing this one

or this one's state,

saying

this one is

a fire-worshipper,

a duality believer,

and so

this one is

hated.

But,

the one

who

is

of the

second circle

sees this one

in that state

where

the One

Who

is

the Sustainer,

sustains.

And

the one

who

is in

the

third circle,

says

that

this one

desires

nothing,

but

aspires

to

Everything.

And

the one

who

has reached

the circle

of

Truth

does not

know

this one

and

disappears

into

the

Beyond.

No place

of refuge

exists,

no way

of escape,

no where

safe…

for

the One

will be

on that day

the refuge..

all will be told,

what they took,

what they gave.

But,

that man turns

to gossip,

to

what others say

to one another…

that man

looks

for a hiding place

fearing sparks,

that man

was deceived,

was in the fire,

now

in

deep danger.

In

the sea

of

Eternity's depths

this one is

absorbed,

and one

who Truth's circle

reaches,

on shore of

in knowledge's sea

is absorbed.

That man

this one

cannot see.

And

of the two birds

the Sufis

kept,

this one

was one.

And,

the other

had two wings,

and

when it

was unable

to fly

again,

it

denied

this one.

That bird

asked

this one:

"What is purity?"

And,

this one said:

"Cut off

your wings

with the knife

of

annihilation…

if not,

you

cannot

follow

this one."

And

that man

said to

this one:

"With these wings

I fly!"

I replied:

"Ah, poor you!

For there is none

like the One,

Who hears all,

sees all."

That man

then fell into

meaning's ocean,

understanding's sea,

and drowned.

Understanding's ocean

could be depicted

as a circle.

With this one's

inner eye

this one saw the One

and this one asked:

"Who are You?"

The One replied:

"You!

So,

where... cannot be

without you

for where

is

nowhere!

And,

the world

cannot judge you

ultimately,

that

is impossible.

You are

the one

who

is everywhere

and

there is no

everywhere.

So,

where

are you?"

A single

point that is drawn

in the circle

by

the power

of

judgment

and

understanding

.

This one point

is the Truth

all else is

in error.

And,

that one*

passed the night

and that one

came closer

to the One.

That one

was away

when seeing

the One

yet not absent.

How

present and not,

looked and did not?

*Note: Prophet Mohammed.

That one

enters the plane

of amazement

and

understands

and

wonder increases.

The One

sees that one

and

that one

sees

the One.

They unite

then separate.

Desire

is attained,

separated from heart.

Heart agrees with

vision.

At first

the One

concealed

that one,

then

drew that one

nearer.

First

empowerment

then

purification,

thirst

then

quenching,

curing

then

caring...

purification

then

glorification,

suffering

then

aiding,

protecting

and

preserving,

then

the One

made

that one

the rider

of

the inner

planes.

That one

became as close

as one

bows-length...

then saw

and

was in act and form

the same.

And,

that one

when called,

responded…

then meditated

was effaced,

when drinking

was satisfied…

when closer

was awestruck…

and

that one

stayed away

from cities,

friends and helpers,

companions,

everyone…

and

that one

transcended

all

symbols,

all

mysteries

and

secrets.

That companion

of yours

never went

away

or astray

or was misled,

never

was tired

or eye tempted

to leave,

and

that one

was

not

sorrowful.

And,

that companion

of yours

never went

away

or astray

or was mislead

from the One

and

in the garden

of memories

never left

the One

and

never lost

the way

in meditating.

That one

was

remembering

the One

with every

breath

with each eye's

blink,

in every

thought,

and

always grateful

for

every sorrow

and

every

blessing.

All

this is…

is

revelation,

inspiration

that

is

revealed

to that one

from

the One..

all Light

to light

from

End

to

end.

That one

gave meaning

to the Word

of

the One...

was detached

from

all created beings,

became

Love

of love

and said:

"Be the bird

of the

highest mountain,

deepest cavern...

highest of meaning,

in peace and helpfulness,

so,

that you

see what

you

have been

created

to be,

destined

to see,

then be

the sword

most sharp

drawn

from the *Kaaba*,

home

of Divinity.

And,

the One

then

was near

that one,

the Truth...

then

the One

was limited

from the Essence,

then

through states and planes

the One

travelled

and came near

that quest,

coming down,

came closer to

that one

who was called...

and came down,

closer to that one.

And

came down

as the One

closer

to that one…

that one who sees

that witness,

came

back down

for all

of us.

And so,

that one

became

the idea

of two bow-lengths,

and

the

question

of

where?

That one was

annihilated

by

separation's arrow,

and

distance was

no more.

And,

all of this

is so,

and

the question of where

is

where?

And,

so much

closer

is

the Essence

of

the essence.

And this one,

Mansur Hallaj,

this one

knew this.

And

only

that one

would

understand

this…

who

the second bow

drew,

and

the second bow

is

beyond

the

Tablet.

And,

there are more letters

there

than the Arabic

or

Persian tongue.

And,

yet…

there is

but one letter

there,

with all…

the letter 'm'.

And,

'm' is the name

of

that one

revealing

all.

And,

that one

is called

the

Last

of all.

And,

of

the

First Bow

that one

is…

the cord.

And

that one

said that the art

of speech

is in its

closeness

to meaning,

and so…

meaning

is the best way

to find the Truth…

not all can take it,

being close means

having to be

held back

in the circle.

So,

what is Reality?

It is

that point

where any link

to the illusory world

no longer exists,

no more

pain

or

sorrow.

It

explains and guides,

It...

is the word

for salvation,

deliverance,

It leads

one

in the Way

and

all then respect

It.

And,

being close

the meaning

is

preserved,

and

is known

only by

who knows,

who is

a loyal pilgrim

on path

to that one…

Messenger

of

the One.

The Master of Medina*

proclaimed glory

of those whose grace,

is in

the 'hidden' Book

preserved…

in all books written,

in those who interpret

speech of birds,

and

that one

is near us

two bows-lengths

or closer,

so the object

of one's sight

is

the Essence.

*Note: The Prophet Mohammed.

O devotee,

if you want

to understand,

know this...

the Master

does not talk

to whom

does not

deserve to hear

that one's

words...

all real talk

is between

the one

who deserves

and

that one.

To be one

of that one's

is to have no master,

for that one

has no disciple,

or authority.

That one

betrays no one,

warns no one,

has no one or thing.

What that one has

that one only has,

or does not have.

That one

is a desert

in a desert,

sign

in a sign.

Meaning

comes only from

that one…

because meaning

from that one

gains hope,

but…

hope is far away

and many dangers

are on way to it.

The name of

that one

is in glory

written.

The form

of

that one

is

unique.

That one

can be see in all,

and being in all

to be seen

is the unity

of

the Reality

to be seen.

That one's

worth, strength, promise

is our pact...

that one's

name, sign, way, fire,

and our desire

for that one

is all of worth,

only to know

that one.

Name of

that one

is to praise,

and arena of

that one

is

suns of all

of the universe,

that one is

light.

And,

all people, towns, cities,

and all who live there

live in

that one's

house…

one family.

And,

the life and being of

that one

are known,

and

that one's

state

is absorption

in the One

and

when manifesting

is self-effacing.

That one's

garden

is full of roses,

and all its paths are

that one's.

And

all who are with

that one

are in the tribe of lovers

and

by love's sign

are recognized,

and

that one

is generous,

as all know,

and all following

that one

reach home.

But,

that one's sorrow

is great.

And,

whatever

that one did say,

forever was said…

is always so,

always will stay.

And,

the glory

is this,

our surety

is this...

all else

is ignorance,

the wilderness,

with no way,

no

destination.

There is no path,

no mission

except that of

that one,

Mohammed...

and only

to that one

the One

has appeared

in many a vision

within

Vision.

And,

Iblis

was by vision

of self

stopped.

Iblis

was told

to bow down

to

that one

and

Mohammed

did not look.

not right,

not left,

not north…

eye

never swerving,

never

was it

going astray.

And

Iblis

was claiming

power,

but

could not

make self

free

from

the self,

from

the power

that was

claimed

at first...

that path.

And,

Mohammed

made claim

to

the mission

and

beyond

the

finite

was

going

and

beyond

the self…

not

ever

compromising.

And

that one

by doing so

revealed

the word:

"Through

You

I move,

upon You

I rely!

O You

Who

all hearts move,

who can fully

praise You?"

And,

of all

in

heaven

there was none

then

superior

to

Iblis

who

knew

the One

was

the

only

One.

And

Iblis saw

the One

then

gave away

that sight,

gave away

the path

to

the One.

Iblis

began

to worship

the One

as

Non-Being,

the Beyond.

And,

on

becoming

individualized,

Iblis

was questioned

then condemned,

and

then

Iblis

begged

to be taken

before

the One.

The One

commanded

Iblis:

"Bow down

before

that one!"

Iblis said:

"There is no other

than

You!"

The One

said:

"You

are cursed!"

Iblis said:

"There is no other

than You!

My disobedience

is because of

Your Purity

and

my reason

is now mad

for You...

Adam

is no other

but

You,

and

between

You and I

is no other,

243

so

I am You!

The only path

for me

is to You,

directly."

The One

replied:

"Your pride

is too much!"

Iblis replied:

"Only now

have I compared

myself

with You...

but

I am proud

for I knew

You

before All began,

before Time.

I was then

preferred

above all others

and I was

obedient

before any other

became obedient.

So,

You incline towards me

and I to You,

an ancient

leaning.

So,

why should I

bow before

that one

who

is not You…

is

other than You?

So,

I had to disobey,

no other choice

was mine.

I

was created

of fire,

to fire

I must return.

You

have the power,

do what You

must do!

From You,

for me

there is

no separation,

no nearness,

we

are one.

But,

I have now

gone far from You,

companion

of my fate.

Such is love,

yet

it appears

to be

separation."

And

on Sinai

Moses met Iblis

and asked:

"Why did you not

bow down?"

Iblis replied:

"I was convinced

that the One

was the only One.

If I had bowed

before that one

I would be

like you,

told to look

towards the mountain

and you did so.

And

I was told

a thousand times

to bow down

before

that one,

Adam…

but

I did not

bow down

because

of what

I did

believe in,

stopped me."

Moses replied:

"You disobeyed

the One's

command?"

Iblis said:
"It was a trial,
not a command!"

Moses replied:
"But,
your face and form
was changed
by this sin."

Iblis said:
"O Moses,
all this is a disguise,
and what is true
never
changes.
What was then
is so now.
That which was real
is still so."

Moses asked:
"Do you
remember the One
now?"

"Does one who
is pure
need to remember?
I am
the remembered
and the One
is remembered.
In our remembering
we are one.
What I do now
is more pure
and I am serving
through
all my days,
and
how I remember
is most glorious
and the One

now remembers

through

me

and I serve

with all my joy

the One.

And,

I no longer desire

to gain or lose…

and so

I am unique

and

will remain so.

And,

the One

then expelled me

from others

who are free

made me into

a different shape

and so

confused

me.

And

the One

imprisoned me,

and

because I praised

the One

allowed me

to fall.

I was kept

far off

because of

my act...

blinded too.

And

I was forsaken,

banished

from

all.

And,

I was not

in error

in my actions

for or against

the One.

I was not proud

of my new form.

Though

I am in the fire

I will

not bow

to that one

only to

the One.

I am

of

the sincere."

The opinions

on Azazil[*]

are many...

upon his state in heaven

and upon earth,

in heaven

to the Angels

he preached

to see good,

upon earth

to see evil.

*Note: Azazil is the name of Iblis (Satan) before his Fall.

Good

is known

due to evil

and evil is known

due to good.

And this one,

Mansur Hallaj, said:

"I argued

with Iblis and Pharaoh

on being faithful,

steadfast.

Iblis said:

'To bow

before Adam

would have been

dishonourable.'

Pharaoh said:

'To believe

that Messenger

would have been

dishonourable

before the others.'

I replied

to them:

'If I too

went back

upon what I

believed,

my faith,

my words,

my teaching,

I would

also

have been

not true

to

myself.'

And

then Iblis said:

'I am better

than Adam

and the One

could

only see

the One.'

Pharaoh said:

'I know

they have no god

but me...

and none

can tell

the real

from

the false.'

And,

I said:

'If the One

you do not recognize,

at least see

the One's

sign...

I am

the everlasting sign

of the One…

I am the Truth

(Anal-Haqq)

and

I am

always

the

Truth.'

And so,

Iblis and Pharaoh

are this one's

helpful companions.

Iblis was burnt

and never changed…

Pharaoh drowned

and never changed.

But,

Pharaoh said:

'I believe in no god

but the One

Israel's children follow.'

The One's sign

was there when Gabriel

made Pharaoh

feel the sand

at water's depth.

And so,

if this one

should be killed,

or

placed on

a gibbet

alive,

or

hands and feet

cut off…

even then

this one

would never

retract

what this one

has stated."

And,

the name of Iblis

came from Azazil,

changed:

'A'...

tireless Action,

'Z'...

Zealous in visiting,

'A'...

Alpha in the ranks,

'Z'...

Zenith in the ranks,

'I'...

Interrupted painful path,

'L'...

Limitless in taking pain.

The One

asked Iblis:

"O fallen one

why would you

not bow?"

The reply was:

"I am a lover

and we are cursed,

and You say

I have fallen...

I have taken

from the Books

of Knowledge

and Light...

O most powerful One,

how could this

happen to me?

So,

how could I bow

to Adam,

when I was created

of fire

and that one

of earth?

Opposites

do not agree,

can they be united?

I have been
obeying and serving
You
so much longer,
being
loved longer,
I am the wiser,
existed longer."

And,
the One
replied:
"I can choose
not you!"

Iblis said:
"Each choice
and my choice
is Yours,
because You
made my choice,
my Creator.

It was Your Will,

O most-powerful One.

If You

had willed I bow

I would have.

Among the wise

I know You

more than any other.

So,

don't blame me,

Your criticism

is not correct payment,

O Master,

as I can't be replaced

in faithfulness.

Your promise,

is most true...

my actions strong...

all should know

that I am

a witness,

a martyr!"

So,

brother...

he was called

Azazil

for he saw himself

as separated

from the original

Pure Source.

And,

he lost his state,

and

did not return,

for he never left

his end...

from his

beginning

cursed.

And,

his attempt

to leave

never worked,

for his character

was flawed.

He discovered
he was caught
in the fire of his zeal,
unbending…
and the light
of his
detachment.

O Brother,
understand this
and you will
understand
the narrowness
of the path,
you
will know
yourself.

If not,
you would find
separation,
detachment,
grief,

bitterness,

worry,

death.

All wise ones

were silent about Iblis

and all who understood,

held their tongues

about it.

Iblis knew

what to bow meant

and

was nearer to

the One

than them,

more loyal in faith

before

the One.

And

they all bowed

before Adam,

they all

obeyed,

and

Iblis refused

for

by the sight of

the One

he had for long

become one

without sight.

And,

in the end

when he

was confused

and lost all

hope of reward

he said:

"I am better

than

that one!"

And

forever

he was veiled

from the dust,

damned,

suffered

from end to End.

The first circle

is the circle

of the Will of the One...

the second circle

is the circle

of the Wisdom

of the One...

the third circle

is the circle

of the Power

of the One...

the fourth circle

is the circle

of the Knowledge,

neverending

of the One.

Iblis said:

"If I entered

the first circle

there was a test

causing death

in the second…

and

in the second

there was a test

causing death

in the third…

and

in the third

there was a test

causing death

in the fourth…

so,

no, no, no,

no…

I stopped

in the first circle

and

I was cursed

until I entered

the second circle,

and

I was cursed

until I entered

the third circle,

so...

why even think

of

the fourth circle?

If I had known

that

to bow down

would free me,

I would have

bowed

before Adam.

But,

I knew only

of circles

in circles...

endlessly.

So,

inwardly I said:

'If I come out

of this first circle

what of the other

circles?'

O

You,

the

First,

the

One,

the only

One

Who

never

dies...

the Living

God...

how?

How?

How?"

The One

is the Truth,

the only One,

unique,

One,

indivisible.

Oneness

and

Knowledge,

Unity

is owned

by

the One,

is in

the

One.

Impossible

to know,

It is

the

beyond,

Beyond...

the Beyond

that

separates

others

from

the

Unity

of

the

One.

Knowledge

of the Oneness,

the Truth,

is

abstract

knowledge...

beyond separation,

indivisible.

To say

'Oneness'

and to say

'The One'

is an attribute,

but the One

is beyond

attributes.

If I should say

'I',

the One

will

reply

'I'

to my

'I'.

So,

my Oneness

comes from

me

and

not the One.

The One

is free

of me.

And,

if I say

'The Oneness

returns to the Unity

who says it,'

then I have made

the One

to be alone,

in creation,

among created beings.

And if I say

'No,

the One

is one in number',

how can

the One

be a number?

And,

if I say,

'The Oneness

is the One,

for the One

is thought of

as only one,

having been proven

to be one,

attaching

the Subject

to the object...'

then

I have made

the One

limited,

defined.

All mystery

creates awe

leading

to the One...

for the One

created it,

bit by

bit.

Secret of

the Oneness

is known

in pronouns:

concealed...

hidden in the Hidden.

The One

is in the one,

and not in the one:

is... not!

If

you or I

say...

"Hah!"

Others wail:

"Ah, ha!"

So many

indications,

so many

creations,

so many

indications

of the One,

yet

the One

still is...

unknown!

The Truth

is

the abode

of

the One,

not

the One.

Saying the Oneness

does not

make

It

exist

in creation.

So,

how to define

the Truth?

And,

if one says:

"The Oneness

is from

the One,"

then one

doubles the One,

the Divine Essence

and

one makes another

other

than the One,

being

and

not being

from

the Essence.

And,

if one says:

"It was hidden

in the One

and

the One

It manifested,"

where,

what,

is It?

What

and where

cannot

contain

the One.

Where and what

are creations

of

the One.

Essence

must have

a subject…

that,

without form

has form,

that

without spirit

has

spirit.

So,

Oneness

is

the Uniter.

And so,

we return

to

the Uniter...

all additions,

all numbers,

all known,

all recognized,

all broken,

all fragmented...

everything.

In

the first circle

are the acts

of

the One...

on points

of

the second circle

are the

points,

traces of

the actions,

marking

the world,

the universe,

the creation.

The inner circle

is the symbol

for the Oneness,

independent,

whole.

And,

this circle

is

the form,

Its form.

And so,

It

is the circle,

made of numbers,

people of all ages

of all lands,

all the seekers,

the followers

and

the lovers.

The first circle

is

of appearances…

second circle

inside it

is

of inner feelings…

third circle

inside it

is

the innermost.

This

is of all things

in creation…

moving,

exciting,

answering,

confusing,

fragmenting.

It

moves

in the circles,

in human consciousness,

when anxious,

when bewildered,

when wondering,

when changing,

when unhappy,

when wandering

in

valleys.

All this

and

all created,

moment to moment

the Truth

transcends

all

remains pure,

beyond

all.

And,

if one says:

"That One

is,"

there is

no argument

on the Oneness,

the Unity.

And,

if one says:

"The

Oneness

of the One

is manifested,

is known,"

then

one is told:

"It,

is true!"

And,

if one says:

"It,

is beyond Time,"

they will say:

"It,

is in all,"

and…

what is inside

can't contain

the Truth,

they believe.

They don't

understand

the Truth,

nor the creation's

numbers,

bringing

limitation.

And,

if One

and Oneness

is added to

by any number,

One

becomes something

from

the illusion

and the Truth

is not of it.

The Truth

is One…

only One.

What is true,

what is illusion,

is not

from

the

Essence.

And,

if one says:

"Oneness,

the One...

is

the

Word,"

the Word

that is

revealed

is

the attribute

of the Essence

not the Essence

in

Itself.

And,

if one says:

"Oneness

means that

the One

wishes

It to be

One,"

the will

or the act

makes it be

an attribute,

or

a created thing

in

the illusion,

the

creation.

And,

if one says:

"The One

is

the

Oneness,

the

Essence

Itself,"

the One

becomes

the

Highest

becomes

the

Oneness

the only

One,

the

Essence.

And,

if one says:

"That one

is not

the

One,"

that one

is seen as

created.

And,

if one says:

"The name

and

the named

are

the same,"

then

the Oneness

is

not there.

And,

if one says:

"The One

is One,"

then

one says

that

the One

is

the essence

of

the Essence

and

the One

is

the

only

One.

This

is the state

where

cause is not...

this

is the state

where

creation is...

circles

make

other circles,

the known

to

the unknown

is moving.

The first circle

is

the Beginning,

Pre-Eternity…

from which all things

come…

the second circle

is

the mind,

thoughts of things,

understanding…

the third circle

is

the dimensions…

the fourth circle

is

knowledge of all.

The Essence

has no

attributes…

the One

stays

unknowable.

The seeker

opens

door of knowledge,

does not see...

opens

door of purity,

does not see...

opens

door of understanding

does not see...

and,

then that one

enters

through

door of meaning...

and

does not see.

And so,

the One,

the Essence,

is not seen

by any word

or action

or help

on

the

way.

All praise,

all glory

be to

the One

above

all the ones

of knowledge,

and

all the ones

of insight,

and

all the ones

of intuition

who know

the glory

of

the One.

This

is the state

of negation and affirmation

manifesting as image.

First image

is

simple thought

of most,

second image is

thought by few

that creates

the circle

of knowledge

of Truth.

Most

coming and going

dive into the sea

of opinion to do

their thinking...

they sink.

The few
swim the sea
on the water
of understanding,
but...
it dries up
and their
knowledge
becomes
worthless.

The One
transcends
the many and few...
pure, powerful,
independent...
all glory is with
the One.

The One
is all Unity,
beginningless,
endless,

Creator of all,

all-knowing,

the One...

the Merciful,

the Uniter.

In the quality

is the Secret,

in the worth

of the wayfarer...

not known

is the form

or the state of

the wayfarer.

Not helpful

is "How?"

And,

"Where?"

in valley of

Reality

is

nowhere.

Understanding
that without limit
is impossible
for the limited.

The Infinite
is
beyond knowing,
beyond all the senses,
beyond all reason,
beyond explanation.

The Infinite
is
beyond annihilation,
even of the self.

The Infinite
is
beyond the finite
creation...
beyond the self
in the finite creation.

And,

any one

who states:

"I have known

the One

by not knowing

the One,"

is not knowing,

is behind the veil

of ignorance.

And,

any one

who states:

"I have known

the One

by the Name of

the One,"

doesn't know

the One,

for

how can

the One

be separated

from

the Name

of

the

One?

And,

any one

who says:

"I have known

the One

through

the One,"

does not know

the One...

for how can

the One

be unknown,

be two,

any other,

be

the knower?

And,

any one

who says:

"I have known

the One

by the works

of

the One,"

does not know

the One,

for

such a one

has placed

the works

of

the One

above

the One.

And,

any one

who says:

"I have known

the One

through

my helplessness,

my inability

to know

the One,"

is

helpless,

unable

to know

even

oneself,

is

lost.

And,

any one

who says:

"I know

the One

through

knowledge of

the knowledge of

the One

of me,"

knows

only

the knowledge

of

the one,

the self.

And,

any one

who says:

"I know

the One,

through attributes

of

the One,"

never knows,

as they are

only

signs,

only

symbols,

they

only

indicate

the existence

of

the One.

And,

any one

who says:

"I know

the One

by the beginning

and end,

life and death

of all,"

does not know

the One

for how can

the One

beyond

all

have a beginning

or

end?

One rarely knows

how or why

things are

as they are…

how hair

that is black

turns into white,

the form

once young

now is old…

so,

how can one

know

the

Creator,

the

Lord of All…

is it possible?

The heart

of each one

of us

is but

a piece of flesh

beating

in

our breasts...

a finite point

in

the universe,

so...

how can

the One

make of

such a space

a home

of

the Infinite?

Reason

has its limitations:

length,

breadth...

and,

religious law

has its limitations:

traditions,

obligations,

and...

the creation,

the sky and earth,

all of the creatures,

is by

the One

in a state of

limitation,

confined,

encircled.

The One

cannot be known

through that

which has

length or breadth,

the One

cannot be known

in the creation,

in the religious way,

in the inner way,

in the sacred laws...

the One

cannot be known

by any way

that is

limited.

And,

any one

who says:

"I know

the One

through

knowing

the creation,

those

signs of

the One,"

such a one

has declared

oneself

to be greater,

to be higher

than

what one

claims

to

know.

Be careful,

who

the One

is seeking!

What

you really know

makes

who you are.

Partial knowledge

is not

knowledge

of the One.

The real seeker

sees,

the real knowledge

stays.

Knowledge

of the limited,

the finite,

beings and worlds,

extends knowledge

but...

is hidden,

limited to

the finite

from

the Infinite One

Who

stays concealed...

comes near,

returns

to

the Self.

But,

any one

who goes within,

who is in awe,

who is longing

desperately,

from love

for

the One

who is

separated

from

the One,

stays

in

the One's

attention.

Any one

who has

real knowledge

is alone…

and any one

who loves

the One

lives in grief...

and any one

living for

the One

loses everything...

and any one

who closes eyes

is seeing

the One...

Who

helps.

And so,

what is

real knowledge?

It

is...

what

it

is!

And,

what is

the One?

The One

is what

the

One

is!

So,

real knowledge

is

what the One

is!

And,

the One

is

what

real knowledge

is!

The One

is

the One,

and

the One

is

always

the only

One.

Other

than this

is

the work

of any one

without

understanding…

all of the

tales

told by

others,

without

understanding,

wanting

more tales

to tell.

Real knowledge

is sought by

a few seekers…

all the others

are living

safe lives…

taking up

ideas of others,

confused

they become

self-absorbed,

without hope,

acting

without care,

without aim,

confused,

in

the dark.

The one

stays

the One,

the truth

stays the Truth,

the Creator

is

the Creation.

It,

always is

and

remains as so...

and,

do not

worry!

APPENDIX

The Story of Iblis (Azazil) and Adam
From 'The Book of Genesis'
of Shahin of Shiraz

Maulana Shahin (14th century) was a Jewish Persian Poet who composed only *masnavis* in the Persian language but written in the Hebrew script. He was alive in his birthplace of Shiraz during the reign of the Il-khanid sultan of Baghdad Abu Said (1316-1335) at whose court was Obeyd Zakani and Khaju Kermani. He is said to have greatly admired three great *masnavi* writers who came before him, Firdausi, Nizami and Rumi and to have been influenced by Sufism and Mansur Hallaj.

It is quite possible that although he would have lived in the large Jewish quarter of Shiraz at the time, with the liberality that existed in that city of about 100,000 (within the walls and another 100,000 outside) he would most likely have come into contact with other poets living there including Hafiz, Obeyd Zakani, Khaju Kermani and Ruh Attar and Jahan Khatun.

His first epic *masnavi Musa-Nama,* 'The Book of Moses' (10,000 couplets) was composed in 1327 and he followed that with *Ardashir-Nama,* 'The Book of Ardashir and Esther' (9000 couplets) six years later. It would be another 25 years for his last masterpiece to appear in 1358 (when Hafiz was 38), his *Bereshit-Nama,* 'Book of Genesis' (8,700 couplets) from which the following is translated and is an insight into the story of Iblis (Azazil) in Hallaj's *Tawasin.*

He should be remembered as one of the great *masnavi* poets of Iran.

Further Reading...

In Queen Ester's Garden: An Anthology of Judeo-Persian Literature. Translated and with an introduction and notes by Vera Baseh Moreen. Yale University Press New Haven. 2000. (Pages 26-119).
Piercing Pearls: The Complete Anthology of Persian Poetry Vol. One, Translation, Introduction by Paul Smith, New Humanity Books, Campbells Creek, 2007.
Studies in Judeo-Persian Literature by J.P. Asmussen. Brill Publishers Leiden. 1973
History of Iranian Literature by Jan Rypka et al. D. Reidel Publishing Company Holland. 1968. (See page 738).
Hafiz of Shiraz, 3 Volumes by Paul Smith. New Humanity Books, Campbells Creek, 2003-12. (Shahin is a major character in this long novel/biography).
The Poets of Shiraz, Translation & Introduction by Paul Smith, New Humanity Books, Campbells Creek, 2012.

(From 'The Book of Genesis')

Azazil, among elite of celestial sphere was ranked:

a leader of other angels, he was the most learned...

from him there came everything that they did know

because of him the lamp of grace did brightly glow.

There was no other angel who was a greater angel,

as it seemed he was created by the Most Merciful.

He was always obedient and he was always trying

to be of more service... obedience always increasing.

His place where he worshipped was all the heavens

and his only work was in service, continually given.

For years beyond counting he kept serving faithfully:
great wealth of obedience he stored.... all, could see.
He knew the law of the Merciful, also that among all
there... upon anyone, damnation could suddenly fall.
He above others was most exulted, most relied upon
of close ones of His Excellency... that Royal Falcon.
When it came to bowing before Adam, he wouldn't:
he denied of supremacy, this mortal... he... couldn't!
But anyway, in company of other angels, he happily
decided that he would fly down... make the journey.
He flew like the wind... and before Adam he landed,
full of pride, but still his curiosity had been pricked:
he would discover who he who was cursed, might be.
Who, what was he like, he who of obedience was free?
After he arrived he stood away... some distance away;
he couldn't justify why he was neglectful in this way.
All the other angels were flying in, in countless rows,
row after row of them... before Adam each one did go.
Then at Command of the Pure... the Almighty One,
bowing down before Adam, one by one they did come
and rubbed their faces in the dust: happily they went
bowing before Adam, obeying God's commandment.
There was only one who held back... it was Azazil:
he stayed where he was... before Adam he never fell.
Then His Supreme Excellency: "Azazil!" called out,
"Why are you there: confused, lazy, or have a doubt?

Come on, come now and bow for it's My command,

or lying in wait for you misfortune's surely at hand."

Upon hearing that command of God, he did reply...

"O Creator of the huge elephant and the small fly...

who like me possesses such a wealth of everything,

I, who for so long Your every command was doing,

tell me... why should I, bow before a lump of clay?

O Pure Almighty, should this one, me... that, obey?

That, there... is from earth: from pure light is... this!

If I have to bow to clay, something is surely amiss!"

The Almighty One: "O you fool who doesn't know,

this is My command... no more disobedience show!

Did I ask you to explain to Me why this has to be?

Whatever's my commandment you obey! Obey Me!

What business do you have with earth or with fire?

The latter burns and former as foundation I require.

You shouldn't imagine that to earth fire is greater...

for, beyond doubt in Adam's clay is a light... purer.

Although the light of Adam is no light everlasting...

in clay of Adam earth certainly will be transmuting.

Now, listen to Me, fire's no relation to earth: none!

The antidote for fire is earth... for the fire is poison.

O you unfortunate one... to earth, not superior is fire:

your ignorance stops you: understanding you require.

With My Almighty Power four jewels I have created:

in the world there's none better that can be perceived:

First there was wind... then fire, then I created water,
and the fourth is the pure earth, a jewel crystal clear.
The four of these are what makes the world fortunate:
each is well-known... each, as magnificent does rate.
Then once again Azazil spoke: "You, Pure Almighty,
hear, not inferior to the earth is the blazing fire to me:
Tell me... why in the world should a mere clod of earth
be compared to essence of fire, as having more worth?
I am not wanting to be bowing down to one such as it:
why because of... it, should... I, in humility have to sit?
I... I'm much better than Adam in every possible way:
why my head down before... that, should I have to lay?
Not another one but You will I ever bow down before:
such a thought as that thought I never have anymore!
O One Exulted, beyond all imagination... I will never
bow before Adam, even on Resurrection Day. Never!
To this... this sign of servitude, I'll not ever be yielding
because Adam's far less than worthy of my prostrating.
Only One worthy of praise, bowing down to is... You:
not I and not Michael and not even great Gabriel too!"
That moment, he from God's command turned away,
that one became an infidel... from Him, he did stray.
The glory of Azazil, due to God's curse... departed,
because an argument with God shouldn't be started.
With all those acts of obedience he had done before...
those hidden and done openly, small and much more,

the Almighty beyond compare struck him in the face:
"Take all your obedience, accused one, O one so vile,
because on your back is carried your obedience, a pile,
you'll escape My anger and I will punish you lightly:
I now curse you until the Day of Resurrection you see:
from you will come calamities, you'll be a mine of evil
and throughout all of eternity you will be wandering,
full of anger, in pain… working and always suffering.
And, I'll give to you the name of Iblis, the Damned…
and your prayers by Me into insults, will be turned."
The one named Iblis replied: "O Praise of Praises…
sending me from You is greatest calamity I confess!
This is my fate because of Adam and through Adam
now to be trapped in chains of sorrow forever, I am."
Again he pleaded to the Almighty saying… "O You,
You Who are Most Kind and Pure, the Judge… You
Who does not have oppression, injustice as attributes,
You are the source, mine of mercy and justice's roots:
I don't deserve this: why, for a mortal, humiliate me?
O You, far more superior to any imagined possibility,
is this how my countless years of service You repay?
Is this how You pay Your debt to… me? Please say!"
The Almighty One answered by saying: "Vile cheat,
for all services done, what payment stops such a bleat?
Now, tell me what you want and I'll give it to you…
injustice is never an attribute My nature does imbue."

Then Iblis replied, with this: "O One most generous,
since it was because of Adam that this happened, thus
I want him and all his offspring handed over to me,
so through sin and desire I may to lowest make them go!
I'll tempt them with troubles every day and each night,
so that forever they'll remain away from mercy's sight:
by being friends with sin they'll become because of me
the very warp and woof of vice... every evil possibility.
I will carry them all down to me, to the depths of Hell,
becoming my army and my troops of evil... they shall:
and I will never allow them to ever again rest in peace
and what they gain I'll turn into loss, make it decrease;
I'll ambush them from the left and also from the right:
their wanting, desiring, will become their worst plight."
Once more the Almighty Judge to Iblis gave an answer:
"You who are a repulsive, unfortunate infidel, so sinister,
As to your wish concerning them I will grant it, let it be;
so... that evil mind that you have should no longer worry.
But over the Saints and Prophets, O one who's so impure,
you'll never be victorious, they will conquer you... be sure!
I'll watch over each stage they pass through... for they are
the greatest fortune ever and the quarry of every treasure.
And it is upon them that I grant a multitude of favours...
for they will be always working for My sake, not yours."
Then Iblis answered... "Every day and also every night,
I will be hard at work demeaning devotion in their sight...

and Your bounties will no longer be a cause of rejoicing:
Each of them, alone, I'll convince of the good of sinning."
The Almighty One answered: "You tyrant, you evil one,
if you turn their eyes from devotion and it they do shun,
in such difficult times as that, them I will not abandon...
it will be easy for Me, from that, to grant their freedom.
I will make them say that they are sorry and I'll also be
soothing them, flattering them until all return to Me."
Then the persevering Iblis answered... " O Almighty,
I will make them, because of their sins, tongue-tied be...
one after another, I will stop them from their repenting,
out from their hearts... such thoughts I will be sending."
The Almighty One then replied, saying: "O one so evil,
of the extent of our mercy you have no conception still...
You don't know that I'm of all My servants the Forgiver,
and of all the helpless and all the weak I am the Guider.
So you should never be imagining in your black evil heart
that Us and Mercy will ever have any reason to depart!"
Iblis replied to Him... "Listen, I did not know that You
had so much Grace to give to help to see them through:
it is impossible for my tricks to be ultimately successful
for Your help to them all of my power will finally annul;
and I am trapped now and I will always be in torment...
strange, I know they'll be enemies, my soul's opponent,
and will always seek vengeance on me because of You...
and much harm to me they will always, be trying to do!

This way they will be and they will not be turning away
from going into a relationship with me... they will stray.
It is surprising to me that You'll show them such mercy:
nothing but grief and troubles they would get from me!"
Then the Almighty One said: "Since those who are dear
to Me, love Me, what is difficult is easy... do you hear?
I will ignore their sins, each of them... one after the other:
on all of their heads I will rain My Mercy... as, I prefer.
And to Paradise I will bring them all through My Grace,
keeping them all for all of Eternity in that Blessed Place."
Lord of Green Firmament... Kind Master of Generosity,
Lord of Truth, Merciful One, Absolute Sultan, Almighty;
when He'd finished his cursing of that one Iblis of name
He turned and glanced at form of that one named Adam,
and He caressed him with the light of His great favour:
with His Mercy He created a shadow over his exterior.
And when He gave to Adam a soul that would survive...
that Adam of the earth, suddenly leapt up... came alive!
Adam bowed down before the Monarch of the Universe,
rubbed his face in the dirt... then with Him did converse,
saying... "Praise be to God! Lord of Heaven and Earth,
I testify that You are the Only One... Lord of all birth,
and, all not yet created... You always are, and will be...
and, by Your Light the Sun and the Moon, we can see!
You brought me out from this earth in only a moment...
and by Your Holy breath into my form a soul You sent.

It's completely right that You are the Supreme Creator...
as You're omniscient and knowing, Guide most superior.
I completely bow to Your Absolute Power and Might...
for You are the Divine Creator of the day and of night."
Then by decree of God, Adam suddenly did understand
all mysteries, forms of knowledge were at his command.
And to Adam... through this grace and this knowledge,
to be able to understand all the world was his privilege.
All of God's Most Exulted Names he came to know...
and God, preference for him above all others did show.
The Lord nourished Adam with many a generous favour
for He'd created him for good deeds and good behaviour.
Then God said to Adam... "O most pure servant, I have
chosen you out of all the celestial innocents that I have:
and I have created the whole of Creation for you Adam:
drawing your stature like that of the tall cypress... I am.
The wild and the tame animals and the birds and the fish,
the cattle and the sheep... whatever you happen to wish
for, I've created for you... the world's fruit moist and dry
you can take and eat... whatever you should want to try!
And from your offspring Adam I'll make to be coming out
a great many people... from you a multitude will sprout,
and with that multitude I will cover the whole of the Earth
so they will be happy and take delight and know its worth.
because of them I've created every comfort that's possible:
the wet and dry I created to make their souls comfortable.

no prayer that is said by your family will be said in vain,

even if it must go around the Earth and come back again!"

O Shahin, whoever that One, the Lord and the Almighty

may favour... even in the slightest, then that one will be

the favourite one in this world, and favourite in the other:

O Lord, please be most merciful on me, Your poor lover!

MOST 6" x 9" (15 cm x 23 cm) PAPERBACKS PERFECTBOUND...
Most also available in pdf format
Cheapest from: www.newhumanitybooksbookheaven.com
check out our website for prices & full descriptions of each book.

TRANSLATIONS

(NOTE: All translations by Paul Smith are in clear, modern English and in the correct rhyme-structure of the originals and as close to the true meaning as possible.)

DIVAN OF HAFIZ
Revised Translation & Introduction by Paul Smith
This is a completely revised one volume edition of the only modern, poetic version of Hafiz's masterpiece of 791 *ghazals, masnavis, rubais* and other poems/songs. The spiritual and historical and human content is here in understandable, beautiful poetry: the correct rhyme-structure has been achieved, without intruding, in readable (and singable) English. In the Introduction of 70 pages his life story is told in greater detail than any where else; his spirituality is explored, his influence on the life, poetry and art of the East and the West, the form and function of his poetry, and the use of his book as a worldly guide and spiritual oracle. His Book, like the *I Ching*, is one of the world's Great Oracles. Included are notes to most poems, glossary and selected bibliography and two indexes. First published in a two-volume hardback limited edition in 1986 the book quickly went out of print. 542 pages.

PERSIAN AND HAFIZ SCHOLARS AND ACADEMICS WHO HAVE COMMENTED ON PAUL SMITH'S FIRST VERSION OF HAFIZ'S *'DIVAN'*.
"It is not a joke... the English version of ALL the *ghazals* of Hafiz is a great feat and of paramount importance. I am astonished. If he comes to Iran I will kiss the fingertips that wrote such a masterpiece inspired by the Creator of all and I will lay down my head at his feet out of respect."
Dr. Mir Mohammad Taghavi (Dr. of Literature) Tehran.
"I have never seen such a good translation and I would like to write a book in Farsi and introduce his Introduction to Iranians." Mr B. Khorramshai, Academy of Philosophy, Tehran.
"Superb translations. 99% Hafiz 1% Paul Smith."Ali Akbar Shapurzman, translator of many mystical works in English to Persian and knower of Hafiz's *Divan* off by heart.
"I was very impressed with the beauty of these books." Dr. R.K. Barz. Faculty of Asian Studies, Australian National University.
"Smith has probably put together the greatest collection of literary facts and history concerning Hafiz." Daniel Ladinsky (Penguin Books author of poems inspired by Hafiz).

HAFIZ – THE ORACLE
(For Lovers, Seekers, Pilgrims, and the God-Intoxicated).
Translation & Introduction by Paul Smith. 441 pages.

HAFIZ OF SHIRAZ.
The Life, Poetry and Times of the Immortal Persian Poet.
In Three Books by Paul Smith. Over 1900 pages, 3 volumes.

PIERCING PEARLS:
THE COMPLETE ANTHOLOGY OF PERSIAN POETRY
(Court, Sufi, Dervish, Satirical, Ribald, Prison & Social Poetry from the 9th to the
20th century.) Volume One
Translations, Introduction and Notes by Paul Smith. Pages 528.

PIERCING PEARLS: THE COMPLETE ANTHOLOGY OF PERSIAN
POETRY (Court, Sufi, Dervish, Satirical, Ribald, Prison & Social Poetry from the
9th to the 20th century.) Vol. Two
Translations, Introduction and Notes by Paul Smith. Pages 462.

DIVAN OF SADI: His Mystical Love-Poetry.
Translation & Introduction by Paul Smith. 421 pages.

RUBA'IYAT OF SADI
Translation & Introduction by Paul Smith. 151 pages.

WINE, BLOOD & ROSES: ANTHOLOGY OF TURKISH POETS
Sufi, Dervish, Divan, Court & Folk Poetry from the 14th – 20th Century
Translations, Introductions, Notes etc., by Paul Smith. Pages 286.

OBEYD ZAKANI: THE DERVISH JOKER.
A Selection of his Poetry, Prose, Satire, Jokes and Ribaldry.
Translation & Introduction by Paul Smith. 305 pages.

OBEYD ZAKANI'S > MOUSE & CAT ^ ^ (The Ultimate Edition)
Translation & Introduction etc by Paul Smith. 191 pages.

THE GHAZAL: A WORLD ANTHOLOGY
Translations, Introductions, Notes, Etc. by Paul Smith.
Pages 658.

NIZAMI: THE TREASURY OF MYSTERIES
Translation & Introduction by Paul Smith. 251 pages.

NIZAMI: LAYLA AND MAJNUN
Translation & Introduction by Paul Smith. 215 pages.

UNITY IN DIVERSITY
Anthology of Sufi and Dervish Poets of the Indian Sub-Continent
Translations, Introductions, Notes, Etc. by Paul Smith. Pages… 356.

RUBA'IYAT OF RUMI
Translation & Introduction and Notes by Paul Smith. 367 pages.

THE *MASNAVI*: A WORLD ANTHOLOGY
Translations, Introduction and Notes by Paul Smith. 498 pages.

HAFIZ'S FRIEND, JAHAN KHATUN: The Persian Princess Dervish Poet… A
Selection of Poems from her *Divan*
Translated by Paul Smith with Rezvaneh Pashai. 267 pages.

PRINCESSES, SUFIS, DERVISHES, MARTYRS & FEMINISTS:
NINE GREAT WOMEN POETS OF THE EAST:
A Selection of the Poetry of Rabi'a of Basra, Rabi'a of Balkh, Mahsati, Lalla Ded,
Jahan Khatun, Makhfi, Tahirah, Hayati and Parvin.
Translation & Introduction by Paul Smith. Pages 367.

RUMI: SELECTED POEMS
Translation, Introduction & Notes by Paul Smith. 220 pages.

KABIR: SEVEN HUNDRED SAYINGS *(SAKHIS)*.
Translation & Introduction by Paul Smith. 190 pages. Third Edition

SHAH LATIF: SELECTED POEMS
Translation & Introduction by Paul Smith. 172 pages

LALLA DED: SELECTED POEMS
Translation & Introduction by Paul Smith. 140 pages.

BULLEH SHAH: SELECTED POEMS
Translation & Introduction by Paul Smith. 141 pages.

NIZAMI: MAXIMS
Translation & Introduction Paul Smith. 214 pages.

KHIDR IN SUFI POETRY: A SELECTION
Translation & Introduction by Paul Smith. 267 pages.

ADAM: THE FIRST PERFECT MASTER AND POET
by Paul Smith. 222 pages.

MODERN SUFI POETRY: A SELECTION
Translations & Introduction by Paul Smith. Pages 249

LIFE, TIMES & POETRY OF NIZAMI
by Paul Smith. 97 pages.

RABI'A OF BASRA: SELECTED POEMS
Translation by Paul Smith. 102 pages.

RABI'A OF BASRA & MANSUR HALLAJ
~Selected Poems~ Translation & Introduction Paul Smith. Pages 134

SATIRICAL PROSE OF OBEYD ZAKANI
Translation and Introduction by Paul Smith. 212 pages.

KHAQANI: SELECTED POEMS
Translation & Introduction by Paul Smith. 197 pages.

IBN 'ARABI: SELECTED POEMS
Translation & Introduction by Paul Smith. 121 pages.

THE *GHAZAL* IN SUFI & DERVISH POETRY: An Anthology:
Translations, Introductions, by Paul Smith Pages 548.

A GREAT TREASURY OF POEMS
BY GOD-REALIZED & GOD-INTOXICATED POETS
Translation & Introduction by Paul Smith. Pages 804.

MAKHFI: THE PRINCESS SUFI POET ZEB-UN-NISSA
A Selection of Poems from her *Divan*
Translation & Introduction by Paul Smith. 154 pages.

~ THE SUFI RUBA'IYAT ~
A Treasury of Sufi and Dervish Poetry in the *Ruba'i* form,
from Rudaki to the 21st Century
Translations, Introductions, by Paul Smith. Pages… 304.

LOVE'S AGONY & BLISS: ANTHOLOGY OF URDU POETRY
Sufi, Dervish, Court and Social Poetry from the 16th- 20th Century
Translations, Introductions, Etc. by Paul Smith. Pages 298.

RUBA'IYAT OF ANSARI
Translation & Introduction by Paul Smith. 183 pages

THE RUBAI'YAT: A WORLD ANTHOLOGY
Court, Sufi, Dervish, Satirical, Ribald, Prison and Social Poetry in the Ruba'i form
from the 9th to the 20th century from the Arabic, Persian, Turkish, Urdu and English.
Translations, Introduction and Notes by Paul Smith Pages 388.

BREEZES OF TRUTH
Selected Early & Classical Arabic Sufi Poetry
Translations, Introductions by Paul Smith. Pages 248.

THE~DIVINE~WINE: A Treasury of Sufi and Dervish Poetry
(Volume One) Translations, Introductions by Paul Smith. Pages... 522.

THE~DIVINE~WINE: A Treasury of Sufi and Dervish Poetry
(Volume Two) Translations, Introductions by Paul Smith. Pages... 533.

TONGUES ON FIRE: An Anthology of the Sufi, Dervish,
Warrior & Court Poetry of Afghanistan.
Translations, Introductions, Etc. by Paul Smith. 322 pages.

THE SEVEN GOLDEN ODES (QASIDAS) OF ARABIA
(The Mu'allaqat)
Translations, Introduction & Notes by Paul Smith. Pages... 147.

THE QASIDA: A WORLD ANTHOLOGY
Translations, Introduction & Notes by Paul Smith. Pages... 354.

IBN AL-FARID: WINE & THE MYSTIC'S PROGRESS
Translation, Introduction & Notes by Paul Smith. 174 pages.

RUBA'IYAT OF ABU SA'ID
Translation, Introduction & Notes by Paul Smith. 227 pages.

RUBA'IYAT OF BABA TAHIR
Translations, Introduction & Notes by Paul Smith. 154 pages.

THE POETS OF SHIRAZ
Sufi, Dervish, Court & Satirical Poets from the 9th to the 20th
Centuries of the fabled city of Shiraz .
Translations & Introduction & Notes by Paul Smith. 428 pages.

RUBA'IYAT OF 'ATTAR
Translation, Introduction & Notes by Paul Smith. 138 Pages.

RUBA'IYAT OF MAHSATI
Translation, Introduction & Notes by Paul Smith. 150 Pages.

RUBA'IYAT OF JAHAN KHATUN
Translation by Paul Smith with Rezvaneh Pashai
Introduction & Notes by Paul Smith. 157 Pages.

RUBA'IYAT OF SANA'I

Translation, Introduction & Notes by Paul Smith. 129 Pages.

RUBA'IYAT OF JAMI
Translation, Introduction & Notes by Paul Smith. 179 Pages.

RUBA'IYAT OF SARMAD
Translation, Introduction & Notes by Paul Smith. 381 pages.

RUBA'IYAT OF HAFIZ
Translation, Introduction & Notes by Paul Smith. 221 Pages.

GREAT SUFI POETS OF THE PUNJAB & SINDH:
AN ANTHOLOGY
Translations & Introductions by Paul Smith 166 pages.

YUNUS EMRE, THE TURKISH DERVISH:
SELECTED POEMS
Translation, Introduction & Notes by Paul Smith. Pages 237.

RUBA'IYAT OF KAMAL AD-DIN
Translation, Introduction & Notes by Paul Smith. Pages 170.

RUBA'YAT OF KHAYYAM
Translation, Introduction & Notes by Paul Smith
Reprint of 1909 Introduction by R.A. Nicholson. 268 pages.

RUBA'IYAT OF AUHAD UD-DIN
Translation and Introduction by Paul Smith. 127 pages.

RUBA'IYAT OF AL-MA'ARRI
Translation & Introduction by Paul Smith. 151 pages

ANTHOLOGY OF CLASSICAL ARABIC POETRY
(From Pre-Islamic Times to Al-Shushtari)
Translations, Introduction and Notes by Paul Smith. Pages 287.

THE *QIT'A*
Anthology of the 'Fragment' in Arabic, Persian and Eastern Poetry.
Translations, Introduction and Notes by Paul Smith. Pages 423.

HEARTS WITH WINGS
Anthology of Persian Sufi and Dervish Poetry
Translations, Introductions, Etc., by Paul Smith. Pages 623.

HAFIZ: SELECTED POEMS
Translation, Introduction & Notes by Paul Smith. 227 Pages.

'ATTAR: SELECTED POETRY
Translation, Introduction & Notes by Paul Smith. 222 pages.

SANA'I : SELECTED POEMS
Translation, Introduction & Notes by Paul Smith. 148 Pages.

THE ROSE GARDEN OF MYSTERY: SHABISTARI
Translation by Paul Smith.
Introduction by E.H. Whinfield & Paul Smith. Pages 182.

RUDAKI: SELECTED POEMS
Translation, Introduction & Notes by Paul Smith. 142 pages.

SADI: SELECTED POEMS
Translation, Introduction & Notes by Paul Smith. 207 pages.

JAMI: SELECTED POEMS
Translation, Introduction by Paul Smith. 183 Pages.

NIZAMI: SELECTED POEMS
Translation & Introduction by Paul Smith. 235 pages.

RUBA'IYAT OF BEDIL
Translation & Introduction by Paul Smith. 154 pages.

BEDIL: SELECTED POEMS
Translation & Introduction by Paul Smith. Pages... 147.

ANVARI: SELECTED POEMS
Translation & Introduction by Paul Smith. 164 pages.

RUBA'IYAT OF 'IRAQI
Translation & Introduction by Paul Smith. 138 pages.

THE WISDOM OF IBN YAMIN: SELECTED POEMS
Translation & Introduction Paul Smith. 155 pages.

NESIMI: SELECTED POEMS
Translation & Introduction by Paul Smith. 169 pages.

SHAH NI'TMATULLAH: SELECTED POEMS
Translation & Introduction by Paul Smith. 168 pages.

AMIR KHUSRAU: SELECTED POEMS
Translation & Introduction by Paul Smith. 201 pages.

A WEALTH OF POETS:
Persian Poetry at the Courts of Sultan Mahmud in Ghazneh
& Sultan Sanjar in Ganjeh (998-1158)
Translations, Introduction and Notes by Paul Smith. Pages 264.

SHIMMERING JEWELS: Anthology of Poetry Under the Reigns
of the Mughal Emperors of India (1526-1857)
Translations, Introductions, Etc. by Paul Smith. Pages 463.

RAHMAN BABA: SELECTED POEMS
Translation & Introduction by Paul Smith. 141 pages.

RUBA'IYAT OF DARA SHIKOH
Translation & Introduction by Paul Smith. 148 pages.

ANTHOLOGY OF POETRY OF THE CHISHTI SUFI ORDER

Translations & Introduction by Paul Smith. Pages 313.

POEMS OF MAJNUN
Translation & Introduction by Paul Smith. 220 pages.

RUBA'IYAT OF SHAH NI'MATULLAH
Translation & Introduction by Paul Smith. 125 pages.

ANSARI: SELECTED POEMS
Translation & Introduction by Paul Smith. 156 pages.

BABA FARID: SELECTED POEMS
Translation & Introduction by Paul Smith. 164 pages.

POETS OF THE NI'MATULLAH SUFI ORDER
Translations & Introduction by Paul Smith. 244 pages.

MU'IN UD-DIN CHISHTI: SELECTED POEMS
Translation & Introduction by Paul Smith. 171 pages.

QASIDAH BURDAH:
THE THREE POEMS OF THE PROPHET'S MANTLE
Translations & Introduction by Paul Smith. Pages 116.

KHUSHAL KHAN KHATTAK: THE GREAT POET
& WARRIOR OF AFGHANISTAN, SELECTED POEMS
Translation & Introduction by Paul Smith. Pages 187.

RUBA'IYAT OF ANVARI

Translation & Introduction by Paul Smith. 104 pages.

'IRAQI: SELECTED POEMS
Translation & Introduction by Paul Smith. 156 pages.

MANSUR HALLAJ: SELECTED POEMS
Translation & Introduction by Paul Smith. Pages 178.

RUBA'IYAT OF BABA AFZAL
Translation & Introduction by Paul Smith. 178 pages.

RUMI: SELECTIONS FROM HIS *MASNAVI*
Translation & Introduction by Paul Smith. 260 pages.

WINE OF LOVE: AN ANTHOLOGY,
Wine in the Poetry of Arabia, Persia, Turkey & the Indian
Sub-Continent from Pre-Islamic Times to the Present
Translations & Introduction by Paul Smith. 645 pages.

GHALIB: SELECTED POEMS
Translation & Introduction by Paul Smith. Pages 200.

THE ENLIGHTENED SAYINGS OF HAZRAT 'ALI
The Right Hand of the Prophet
Translation & Introduction by Paul Smith. Pages 260.

HAFIZ: TONGUE OF THE HIDDEN
A Selection of *Ghazals* from his *Divan*
Translation & Introduction Paul Smith. 133 pages. Third Edition.

~ HAFIZ: A DAYBOOK ~
Translation & Introduction by Paul Smith. 375 pages.
~ ˙ RUMI ˙ ~ A Daybook
Translation & Introduction by Paul Smith. Pages 383.

SUFI POETRY OF INDIA ~ A Daybook~
Translation & Introduction by Paul Smith. Pages 404.

~ SUFI POETRY~ A Daybook
Translation & Introduction by Paul Smith. Pages 390.

~ ˙ KABIR ˙ ~ A Daybook
Translation & Introduction by Paul Smith. 382 pages.

~ABU SA'ID & SARMAD~ A Sufi Daybook
Translation & Introduction by Paul Smith. 390 pages.

~*SADI*~ A Daybook
Translation & Introduction by Paul Smith. 394 pages.

NIZAMI, KHAYYAM & 'IRAQI ... A Daybook
Translation & Introduction by Paul Smith. 380 pages.

ARABIC & AFGHAN SUFI POETRY ... A Daybook
Translation & Introduction by Paul Smith. 392 pages.

TURKISH & URDU SUFI POETS... A Daybook
Translation & Introduction by Paul Smith. 394 pages.

SUFI & DERVISH RUBA'IYAT (9th – 14th century)
A DAYBOOK
Translation & Introduction by Paul Smith. 394 pages.

SUFI & DERVISH RUBA'IYAT (14thth – 20th century)
A DAYBOOK
Translation & Introduction by Paul Smith. 394 pages.

~SAYINGS OF THE BUDDHA: A DAYBOOK~
Revised Translation by Paul Smith from F. Max Muller's. 379 pages.

GREAT WOMEN MYSTICAL POETS OF THE EAST
~ A Daybook ~ Translation & Introduction by Paul Smit. 385 pages.

ABU NUWAS SELECTED POEMS
Translation & Introduction by Paul Smith. 154 pages.

HAFIZ: THE SUN OF SHIRAZ:
Essays, Talks, Projects on the Immortal Poet
by Paul Smith. 249 pages.

~*NAZIR AKBARABADI*~ SELECTED POEMS
Translation and Introduction Paul Smith. 191 pages.

~RUBA'IYAT OF IQBAL~
Translation & Introduction by Paul Smith. 175 pages.

~*IQBAL*~ SELECTED POETRY
Translation & Introduction by Paul Smith. 183 pages.

>THE POETRY OF INDIA<
Anthology of Poets of India from 3500 B.C. to the 20th century
Translations, Introductions... Paul Smith. Pages... 622.

BHAKTI POETRY OF INDIA... AN ANTHOLOGY

Translations & Introductions Paul Smith. Pages 236.

SAYINGS OF KRISHNA: A DAYBOOK
Translation & Introduction Paul Smith. Pages 376.

~CLASSIC POETRY OF AZERBAIJAN~ An Anthology~
Translation & Introduction Paul Smith. 231 pages.

THE TAWASIN: MANSUR HALLAJ
(Book of the Purity of the Glory of the One)
Translation & Introduction Paul Smith. Pages 264.

MOHAMMED In Arabic, Sufi & Eastern Poetry
Translation & Introduction by Paul Smith. Pages 245.

GITA GOVINDA
The Dance of Divine Love of Radha & Krishna
>Jayadeva< Translation by Puran Singh & Paul Smith. Pages 107.

GREAT WOMEN MYSTICAL POETS OF THE EAST
~ A Daybook ~ Translation & Introduction by Paul Smith. 385 pages.

~SUFI LOVE POETRY~ An Anthology
Translation & Introduction Paul Smith. Pages 560.

HUMA: SELECTED POEMS OF MEHER BABA
Translation & Introduction Paul Smith. Pages 244.

RIBALD POEMS OF THE SUFI POETS
Abu Nuwas, Sana'i, Anvari, Mahsati, Rumi, Sadi and Obeyd Zakani
Translation & Introduction Paul Smith. 206 pages.

FIVE GREAT EARLY SUFI MASTER POETS
Mansur Hallaj, Baba Tahir, Abu Sa'id, Ansari & Sana'i
SELECTED POEMS
Translation & Introduction by Paul Smith. Pages 617

FIVE GREAT CLASSIC SUFI MASTER POETS
Khaqani, Mu'in ud-din Chishti, 'Attar & Auhad ud-din Kermani
SELECTED POEMS
Translation & Introduction Paul Smith. Pages 541.

ANTHOLOGY OF WOMEN MYSTICAL POETS
OF THE MIDDLE-EAST & INDIA
Translation & Introduction Paul Smith. Pages 497.

FOUR MORE GREAT CLASSIC SUFI MASTER POETS
Sadi, 'Iraqi, Yunus Emre, Shabistari.
SELECTED POEMS
Translation & Introduction Paul Smith. Pages 562.

~ANOTHER~
FOUR GREAT CLASSIC SUFI MASTER POETS
Amir Khusrau, Ibn Yamin, Hafiz & Nesimi
SELECTED POEMS Translation & Introduction Paul Smith. Pages 636.

FOUR GREAT LATER CLASSIC SUFI MASTER POETS
Shah Ni'mat'ullah, Jami, Dara Shikoh & Makhfi
···SELECTED POEMS···
Translation & Introduction Paul Smith. Pages 526.

THE FOUR LAST GREAT SUFI MASTER POETS
Shah Latif, Nazir Akbarabadi, Ghalib and Iqbal
···SELECTED POEMS···
Translation & Introduction Paul Smith. Pages 616.

'ATTAR & KHAQANI: SUFI POETRY ~A Daybook~
Translation & Introduction Paul Smith. 388 pages.

POET-SAINTS OF MAHARASHTRA:
SELECTED POEMS
Translations & Introductions by Paul Smith. Pages 198.

ABHANGS & BHAJANS OF THE GREATEST INDIAN
POET-SAINTS
Translations & Introductions Paul Smith. Pages 214.

A TREASURY OF LESSER-KNOWN GREAT SUFI POETS
Translation & Introduction Paul Smith. Pages 736.

HATEF OF ISFAHAN AND HIS FAMOUS TARJI-BAND
Translation & Introduction Paul Smith. Pages 129.

CLASSIC BATTLE POEMS OF ANCIENT INDIA
& ARABIA, PERSIA & AFGHANISTAN
Translation & Introduction Paul Smith. Pages 246.

~ANOTHER~ FIVE GREAT CLASSIC SUFI MASTER POETS
Ibn al-Farid, Ibn 'Arabi, Baba Farid, Baba Afzal, Rumi.
SELECTED POEMS
Translation & Introduction Paul Smith. Pages 626.

ANTHOLOGY OF GREAT SUFI & MYSTICAL POETS OF PAKISTAN
Translation & Introduction by Paul Smith. Pages 260.

ZARATHUSHTRA: SELECTED POEMS
A New Verse Translation and Introduction by Paul Smith
from the Original Translation by D.J. Irani.
Original Introduction by Rabindranath Tagore. 141 pages.

THE DHAMMAPADA: The Gospel of the Buddha
Revised Version by Paul Smith
from translation from the Pali of F. Max Muller. 247 pages

THE YOGA SUTRAS OF PATANJALI
"The Book of the Spiritual Man" An Interpretation By Charles Johnston,
General Introduction by Paul Smith. Pages 173.

BHAGAVAD GITA: The Gospel of the Lord Shri Krishna
Translated from Sanskrit with Introduction by Shri Purohit Swami,
General Introductions by Charles Johnston Revised into Modern English
with an Introduction by Paul Smith. 326 pages.

~TAO TE CHING~ by Lao Tzu
Modern English Version by Paul Smith
from the Translation from the Chinese by Paul Carus. Pages 147.

THE PERSIAN ORACLE: Hafiz of Shiraz
Translation, Introduction & Interpretations by Paul Smith
Pages 441.

CAT & MOUSE: Obeyd Zakani
Translation & Introduction by Paul Smith
7" x 10" Illustrated 183 pages

HAFEZ: THE DIVAN
Volume One: The Poems
Revised Translation Paul Smith
"7 x 10" 578 pages.

HAFEZ: THE DIVAN
Volume Two: Introduction
Paul Smith
7" x 10" 224 pages.

~ SAADI ~ THE DIVAN
Revised Translation & Introduction Paul Smith
7" x 10" 548 pages.

~Introduction to Sufi Poets Series~

Life & Poems of the following Sufi poets, Translations & Introductions: Paul Smith

AMIR KHUSRAU, ANSARI, ANVARI, AL-MA'ARRI, 'ATTAR, ABU
SA'ID, AUHAD UD-DIN, BABA FARID, BABA AZFAL, BABA TAHIR,
BEDIL, BULLEH SHAH, DARA SHIKOH, GHALIB, HAFIZ, IBN 'ARABI,
IBN YAMIN, IBN AL-FARID, IQBAL, INAYAT KHAN, 'IRAQI, JAHAN
KHATUN, JAMI, KAMAL AD-DIN, KABIR, KHAQANI, KHAYYAM,
LALLA DED, MAKHFI, MANSUR HALLAJ, MU'IN UD-DIN CHISHTI,
NAZIR AKBARABADI, NESIMI, NIZAMI, OBEYD ZAKANI,
RAHMAN BABA, RUMI, SANA'I, SADI, SARMAD, SHABISTARI,
SHAH LATIF, SHAH NI'MAT'ULLAH, SULTAN BAHU, YUNUS
EMRE, EARLY ARABIC SUFI POETS, EARLY PERSIAN SUFI POETS,
URDU SUFI POETS, TURKISH SUFI POETS, AFGHAN SUFI POETS 90
pages each.

POETRY

THE MASTER, THE MUSE & THE POET
An Autobiography in Poetry by Paul Smith. 654 Pages.

~A BIRD IN HIS HAND~
POEMS FOR AVATAR MEHER BABA
by Paul Smith. 424 pages.

PUNE: THE CITY OF GOD (A Spiritual Guidebook to the New Bethlehem)
Poems & Photographs in Praise of Avatar Meher Baba
by Paul Smith. 159 pages.

COMPASSIONATE ROSE
Recent *Ghazals* for Avatar Meher Baba by Paul Smith. 88 pages.

~THE ULTIMATE PIRATE~ (and the Shanghai of Imagination)
A FABLE by Paul Smith. 157 pages.

+THE CROSS OF GOD+
A Poem in the *Masnavi* Form
by Paul Smith (7 x 10 inches).

RUBA'IYAT ~ of ~ PAUL SMITH
Pages 236.

SONG OF SHINING WONDER
& OTHER *MASNAVI* POEMS
Paul Smith. Pages 171.

~TEAMAKER'S *DIVAN... GHAZALS*~
Paul Smith. Pages 390.

CRADLE MOUNTAIN
Paul Smith... Illustrations – John Adam. (7x10 inches) Second Edition.

~BELOVED & LOVER~
Ghazals by Paul Smith... inspired by Meher Baba Pages 410.

POEMS INSPIRED BY 'GOD SPEAKS' BY MEHER BABA
Paul Smith... Pages 168.

MEHER BABA'S SECLUSION HILL
Poems & Photographs by Paul Smith "7 x 10" 120 pages.

FICTION

THE FIRST MYSTERY A Novel of the Road...
by Paul Smith. 541 pages.

~THE HEALER AND THE EMPEROR~
A Historical Novel Based on a True Story
by Paul Smith Pages 149.

>>>GOING<<<BACK...
A Novel by Paul Smith. 164 pages.

THE GREATEST GAME
A Romantic Comedy Adventure With A Kick!
by Paul Smith 187 pages.

GOLF IS MURDER! A Miles Driver Golfing Mystery
by Paul Smith. 176 pages.

THE ZEN-GOLF MURDER! A Miles Driver Golfing Mystery
by Paul Smith 146 pages.

~RIANA~ A Novel by Paul Smith 154 pages.

CHILDREN'S FICTION

PAN OF THE NEVER-NEVER
by Paul Smith 167 pages.

~HAFIZ~
The Ugly Little Boy who became a Great Poet

by Paul Smith 195 pages.

SCREENPLAYS

>>>GOING<<<BACK...
A Movie of War & Peace Based on a True Story ...
Screenplay by Paul Smith

HAFIZ OF SHIRAZ
The Life, Poetry and Times of the Immortal Persian Poet.
A Screenplay by Paul Smith

LAYLA & MAJNUN BY NIZAMI
A Screenplay by Paul Smith

PAN OF THE NEVER-NEVER ...
A Screenplay by Paul Smith

THE GREATEST GAME
A Romantic Comedy Adventure With A Kick!
A Screenplay by Paul Smith

GOLF IS MURDER!
Screenplay by Paul Smith

THE HEALER & THE EMPEROR
A True Story... Screenplay
by Paul Smith

THE * KISS ... A Screen-Play
by Paul Smith

THE ZEN-GOLF MURDER!
A Screenplay by Paul Smith

TELEVISION

HAFIZ OF SHIRAZ:
A Television Series
by Paul Smith

THE FIRST MYSTERY
A Television Series For The New Humanity
by Paul Smith

THE MARK: The Australian Game

A Thirteen-Part Doco-Drama for Television   by Paul Smith

PLAYS, MUSICALS

HAFIZ: THE MUSICAL DRAMA
by Paul Smith

THE SINGER OF SHIRAZ
A Radio Musical-Drama on the Life of Persia's Immortal Poet,
Hafiz of Shiraz by Paul Smith

ART

MY DOGS
From the Sketchbooks of Gus Cohen. 8″ x 10″ 224 pages

A BRIDGE TO THE MASTER … MEHER BABA
Paintings & Drawings, Poems & Essays by Oswald Hall
Edited & Introduction by Paul Smith   8″ x 10″ 337 pages.

MY VIEW
From the Sketchbooks of Gus Cohen, Barkers Creek Castlemaine
8″ x 10″ 210 pages.

KARL GALLAGHER: PAINTINGS & POETRY 150 pages.

"To penetrate into the essence of all being and significance
and to release the fragrance of that inner attainment
for the guidance and benefit of others, by expressing
in the world of forms, truth, love, purity and beauty…
this is the only game which has any intrinsic and absolute
worth. All other, happenings, incidents and attainments can,
in themselves, have no lasting importance."
Meher Baba

CPSIA information can be obtained
at www.ICGtesting.com
Printed in the USA
BVOW04s0222190617
487245BV00007B/121/P